ICONS

Eric Stanton

Eric Stanton

Reunion in Ropes & Other Stories

TASCHEN

KÖLN LONDON MADRID NEW YORK PARIS TOKYO

X
B.
F.
Stanton

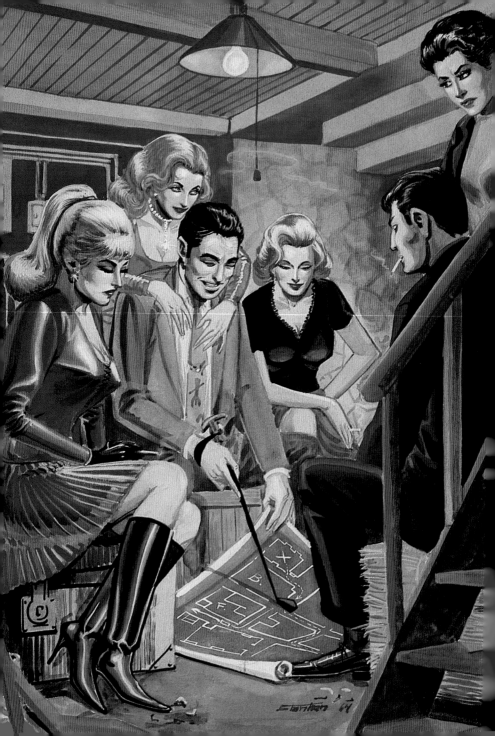

CONTENTS
INHALT
SOMMAIRE

© 2001 TASCHEN GmbH
Hohenzollernring 53, D-50672 Köln
www.taschen.com

© for the illustrations by Britt Stanton, Clinton (CT), USA
Editorial coordination by Nina Schmidt, Cologne
Cover design by Angelika Taschen, Cologne
German translation by Harald Hellmann, Cologne
French translation by Philippe Safavi, Paris

Printed in Italy
ISBN 3-8228-5529-4

THE FETISH KING

In 1976 I took my first job in the sex industry. It was a mild one by industry standards — editorial assistant at a pretentious hardcore magazine called Puritan. Exciting enough for me, however. Every day's mail brought new insights, photos and fiction, and peculiar publications for review. One of the latter was a curious little comic book titled The Punished Publisher, boasting of "81 illustrations by Stanton." I was a fan of the underground comics of R. Crumb and S. Clay Wilson, and thought in them I'd seen every level of perversity, but this Stanton introduced me to worlds undreamt-of. While Crumb's amazons were invariably mastered by his nerdy self-projections, Stanton's kicked butt. In The Punished Publisher, the voluptuous beauties outwit and outwrestle their abusive employer and force him to fellate a monstrous strap-on dildo. To a rather powerless female publishing employee, this was real cool. Feminism was enjoying its powerful first wave in '76, but few men I knew took it seriously. Stanton seemed not only to recognize the feminist struggle, but also to realize that men could be aroused by these strong, angry women, and might harbor a guilty desire to right the wrongs of mankind by submission to female power.

Female sexual power, that is. And to a young feminist foot soldier in the sexual revolution, having sexual power over men was a very appealing prospect. I took Stanton for that creature we used to call a 'male feminist', and added The Punished Publisher to my private collection. It's lying on my desk now as I write this, and in rereading is as amusing to me as a 46-year-old as it was at 24. Except that I know now it's just a superb dominance fantasy and not a political tract. Eric Stanton was full of vision, but even when he was young, sexual politics were the only kind that held his interest.

There were rumors that Stanton, born Ernest Stanzone, enjoyed a wild youth. My favorite bit of lore is that he worked as a knife thrower. He did grow up near the vast, squalid seaside park of Brooklyn's Coney Island, but how did a shy boy acquire a job like that? Had he any skill? And whom or what did he throw these knives at? I suppose the carnival life was even more reckless then than now. As late as 1984, when Stanton would have been close to sixty, I was approached on a New York City street by a man named Paul, who claimed to be recruiting women to wrestle in Eric Stanton videos. I laughed, mainly because I actually knew who Stanton was and imagined the confusion of other women he approached, but also because I couldn't imagine why such a talented artist would be producing wrestling videos. A friend was also accosted by this man with the same pitch. As an out-of-work porn actress and generally fearless creature, she went with him to a nice uptown apartment where she did indeed wrestle another woman. Stanton was not there, but six months later the man I'd met on the street called the office of the crummy magazine then employing me, seeking promotion for a line of Eric Stanton videos. And there in his brochures were the photos of my friend Suzy sitting on another woman's face. I asked Paul why the great Eric Stanton was making wrestling videos, and he said, "Eric likes wrestling." It was clear that that was impetus enough for the wild Mr. Stanton.

When I actually came to know Eric Stanton in 1991 he was in his mid-sixties and I found him a gentle, self-deprecating man, though he still styled his beard and black hair in the satanic style of his cartoon alter ego, Dastardly. I'd often heard him described as reclusive, but that implies something unhealthy and antisocial, and I found him neither. He was simply a family man working at home, steadily producing his illustrations and Stantoons — small, self-published comic books — for a worldwide clientele. I imagine it's the shocking nature of his art that makes people want to find some pathology in his life, but his is a case where the art is not necessarily a window to the soul.

Stanton worked as a commercial fetish artist for 50 years. Ninety percent of his work was done on commission. Because he had a unique talent to take on, get inside, understand and appreciate the fantasies of others, every painting, illustration or comic strip displays a similar creative passion. Thus, there is much confusion over his real-life proclivities. We know he took his early inspiration from John Willie and did credible imitations of Willie's work for Irving Klaw. Viewing this body of work we would assume he loved bondage and female submission. He did elaborately imaginative diagrams of stiletto shoes, à la Willie, and one would assume such brilliant designs could only spring from an obsession with torturous footwear. Then there were all those cross-dressing strips for Female Mimics and other American transvestite magazines in the mid-sixties and early seventies. And what of the mighty − and mighty disturbing − Princkazons, seven-foot women with breasts the size of prize pumpkins and pricks like battering rams? These male/female hybrids delight in overpowering inferior men and forcing them to accommodate their monstrous 'princks'. I asked Eric about these in particular, and he shrugged it off. "It was a private client's idea and I had fun drawing them. Once I'd developed the characters, I thought I'd try them as Stantoons. I've learned if one customer has a fantasy, lots of others usually share it. They've been good sellers."

And what's the significance of the name princk?

"Oh, they're women with pricks, so I wanted to make a special name for the female prick. I put an 'n' in there because that sounds sort of feminine. Like pink." Simple, you see.

So Eric, in rendering every permutation of perversion, concealed as much as he revealed. His own modest quirks are there, but with no flashing lights, no signs distinguishing the personal obsessions from the assumed. This is as he liked it. Not that he wouldn't reveal himself if pressed.

"I have always loved amazons," he once told me. "The word itself is exciting. I've invented variations; Tame-azons who tame men, and the Princkazons. Being short and a little shy as a young man, I loved the idea of big strong aggressive women who would use their strength to wrestle me down and force me to have sex with them. It's a desire to be wanted, that kind of wanting women take for granted from men, but men rarely experience from women. Easy sex, where a woman lies on a bed and you get on top of her, isn't very interesting. I'm a man, I like a struggle, a conquest. I just happen to like being the loser, and then made to satisfy the female winner."

The Stantoons comic books he self-published and marketed since the seventies offer the most insight into Eric the man, because they're some of his only noncommissioned work. Wrestling, either female/female or female/male, appears in almost every one. Even the Princkazons enjoy scissoring their victims before the inevitable penetration. Most matches include Eric's personal favorite, variously called Queening, smother sub-mission or panty smother. Simply, it's a woman sitting astride a man's upturned face, her pantied pudenda securely clamped over his nose and mouth.

Forcing him to satisfy her.

When Eric met future wife Britt in 1971, he was so taken ("You seem to have come out of one of my comics!") he created a public photographic record of his submission to her erotic power. A short film and accompanying stills show the young Norwegian model wrestling the normally shy artist down and sitting triumphantly on his face. His surrender was not simply symbolic; Britt remained his personal Goddess and Demon, dishing up pleasure and pain at her discretion. Eric loved her with the fervor that only a Stanton character could.

In his last years before his death on March 17, 1999, Eric tutored their young daughter in drawing Stanton-style comics. The beautiful teenager shows a special facility for scenes of female dominance, but then, the cruelty of teenage girls is well known. Eric used to chuckle proudly, "Just like her mother."

Stanton claimed that after so many years he no longer minded the public's concocting fantasies about his life, except for the one about him being dead. He complained it let people think they could steal his work with impunity. He found his images, bearing other people's copyright bylines, on shower curtains, stationery and even wallpaper. And there was the continual thorn of that character in England who grew so rich and famous 'sampling' his work that Stanton couldn't afford to sue him ...

Still, Eric Stanton had a long and satisfying life. As he told me once, he had only a single remaining goal. He really wanted to produce the ultimate Stanton Millennium Calendar. It would have been a modest thing for Eric The Wild, but perfectly in scale with gentle, precise Ernest Stanzone, the boy from Brooklyn who would become fetish king.

Dian Hanson, Editor, LEG SHOW Magazine

DER KÖNIG DER FETISCH-WELT

Meinen ersten Job in der Sexindustrie nahm ich 1976 an: Redaktionsassistentin bei einem aufgeblasenen Hardcoremagazin namens Puritan. Für die Branche war meine Arbeit noch relativ harmlos, für mich allerdings schon ganz schön aufregend. Jeden Tag brachte die Post neue Einblicke, Fotos, Storys und Rezensionsexemplare von seltsamen Publikationen. Zu den letzteren zählte auch ein eigenartiges kleines Comicbüchlein mit dem Titel The Punished Publisher, das auf dem Cover stolz verkündete: „81 Illustrationen von Stanton". Nun war ich ein Fan der Undergroundcomics von R. Crumb und S. Clay Wilson und glaubte, bei ihnen schon jeder erdenklichen Spielart von Perversion begegnet zu sein, doch Stanton zeigte mir Welten, die ich mir noch nicht einmal im Traum vorgestellt hätte. Während Crumbs Amazonen doch immer wieder von seinen mickrigen Selbstprojektionen bezwungen wurden, machten die von Stanton jeden zur Schnecke. In The Punished Publisher übertölpeln und überwältigen die üppigen Schönheiten ihren schmierigen Arbeitgeber und zwingen ihn, an einem monströsen Strap-on-Dildo zu lutschen. Auf mich eher machtlose kleine Angestellte eines Verlegers wirkte das natürlich ziemlich cool. Der Feminismus erlebte 1976 seinen ersten Höhepunkt, aber wenige der Männer, die ich kannte, nahmen das ernst. Stanton schien nicht nur den Kampf der Frauen um Selbstbehauptung wahrzunehmen, er schien auch zu begreifen, dass Männer von diesen starken, zornigen Frauen erregt werden konnten und vielleicht ein schuldbewusstes Verlangen danach verspürten, sich der sexuellen Macht der Frau zu unterwerfen.

Als junge, feministische Fußsoldatin der sexuellen Revolution war es für mich eine ausgesprochen attraktive Vorstellung, sexuelle Macht über Männer auszuüben. Ich zählte Stanton zu den Wesen, die wir damals „männliche Feministen" nannten, und

legte The Punished Publisher **in meine kleine Privatsammlung. Während ich dies hier schreibe, liegt das Heft vor mir auf dem Schreibtisch, und es jetzt wieder zu lesen, ist für mich noch genauso amüsant wie damals. Nur dass ich heute weiß, dass es lediglich eine tolle Fantasiegeschichte über Dominanz ist und kein politisches Traktat. Eric Stanton war ein Mann von großer Vorstellungskraft, aber selbst als junger Mann schon konnte nur der Geschlechterkampf seine Fantasie fesseln.**

Es heißt, Stanton, bürgerlich Ernest Stanzone, habe eine wilde Jugend gehabt. Meine Lieblingsgeschichte ist, dass er Messerwerfer gewesen sei. Er wuchs in Brooklyn neben dem riesigen, verwahrlosten Vergnügungspark von Coney Island auf, aber wie hätte ein schüchterner Junge wie er an einen solchen Job kommen können? Hatte er überhaupt Talent dazu? Und auf was oder wen warf er diese Messer? Ich denke mal, damals war das Jahrmarktleben noch riskanter als heute.

1984, da muss Stanton schon fast 60 gewesen sein, wurde ich in New York von einem gewissen Paul auf der Straße angesprochen. Er behauptete, Frauen für Wrestling-Videos von Eric Stanton anzuheuern. Ich lachte, weil der Name Stanton mir zwar etwas sagte, ich mir aber die Verwirrung der anderen Frauen vorstellte, denen er das erzählte. Außerdem war es mir ein Rätsel, warum dieser talentierte Künstler Wrestling-Videos produzieren sollte. Eine meiner Freundinnen wurde von diesem Paul mit derselben Masche angesprochen. Als Ex-Pornodarstellerin und überhaupt von Natur aus furchtlos legte sie tatsächlich mit einer anderen Frau einen Ringkampf hin. Stanton war nicht zugegen, aber sechs Monate später rief Paul bei dem miesen Blättchen an, bei dem ich damals arbeitete, und wollte etwas Promotion für eine Reihe mit Eric-Stanton-Videos. Und in seinen Prospekten sah ich sie wieder: meine Freundin Suzie, wie sie auf dem Gesicht einer anderen Frau saß. Ich fragte Paul, wieso der berühmte Eric Stanton Wrestling-Videos machen würde, und er meinte bloß: „Eric mag Wrestling." Offensichtlich war das für den wilden Mr. Stanton Anlass genug.

Als ich Eric Stanton 1991 schließlich persönlich kennenlernte, war er Mitte 60, und ich erlebte ihn als freundlichen, bescheidenen Menschen, auch wenn er seinen Bart und sein schwarzes Haar immer noch wie ein satanisches Alter ego seines Comic-Helden Dastardley stylte. Er wurde oft als Einsiedler beschrieben, aber damit verbindet man etwas Krankhaftes oder Antisoziales, was ich an ihm nicht entdecken konnte. Er war einfach ein Familienmensch, der zu Hause arbeitete und still und stetig seine Illustrationen und seine „Stantoons" – kleine, selbstverlegte Comic-Hefte – für Leser auf der ganzen Welt produzierte. Das Schockierende seiner Kunst veranlasst die Leute wohl, etwas Pathologisches an ihm entdecken zu wollen, aber in seinem Fall öffnet die Kunst nicht unbedingt ein Fenster zu seiner Seele.

Stanton war 50 Jahre lang als kommerzieller Fetischkünstler tätig. 90% seiner

Arbeiten waren Auftragsarbeiten. Weil er über das einzigartige Talent verfügte, sich die Fantasien anderer Menschen zu Eigen zu machen, sie verstand und respektierte, zeigt jedes seiner Bilder, jede Zeichnung oder jeder Comicstrip die gleiche künstlerische Hingabe. Daher herrscht viel Unklarheit, welche Vorlieben er tatsächlich hatte. Wir wissen, dass er seine ersten Anregungen von John Willie bekam und dessen Stil überzeugend für Irving Klaw imitierte. Wenn man die Mehrzahl seiner Werke betrachtet, könnte man meinen, dass er Bondage und weibliche Unterwerfung liebte. Er hat ausgefeilt fantasievolle Darstellungen von Stilettos à la Willie gezeichnet, und man sollte meinen, dass so brillante Designs nur jemandem gelingen, der eine Obsession für solches Folterschuhwerk pflegt. Aber dann waren da Mitte der 60er bis in die frühen 70er auch all die Transvestitenstrips für Female Mimics und andere amerikanische Transvestitenmagazine. Und was ist mit den mächtigen – und mächtig verstörenden – „Princkazons", den Zwei-Meter-Frauen mit Brüsten wie Wassermelonen und Schwänzen wie Rammböcke? Diese Zwitterwesen finden Spaß daran, hilflose Männer zu überwältigen und zu zwingen, ihre monströsen „Princks" zu schlucken. Ich fragte Eric einmal danach, und er tat es mit einem Achselzucken ab: „Das war die Idee eines privaten Kunden, und es machte Spaß, sie zu zeichnen. Nachdem ich schon mal die Figuren entwickelt hatte, dachte ich, nimm sie doch auch für die ,Stantoons'. Ich weiß aus Erfahrung, dass meistens auch noch viele andere die Fantasie eines Kunden teilen. Und sie haben sich gut verkauft."

„Und warum heißt es ,Princk'?"

„Ach, es sind Frauen mit Schwänzen (pricks), und ich wollte einen speziellen Namen für ihre Schwänze finden. Also fügte ich ein ,n' ein, weil das irgendwie weiblich klingt. Wie in ,pink'. So einfach ist das."

Durch seine Darstellungen sämtlicher möglichen und unmöglichen Perversionen verschleiert Eric also genauso viel wie er offenbart. Seine eigenen kleinen Vorlieben spielen zwar mit hinein, aber sie rufen nicht „Hier!", seine persönlichen Obsessionen sind von anderen, übernommenen, nicht zu unterscheiden. So hat es ihm gefallen. Das heißt nicht, dass er nicht doch etwas offenbart hätte, wenn man ihn drängte.

„Ich habe schon immer Amazonen gemocht", verriet er mir. „Schon das Wort allein ist aufregend. Ich habe mir einige Variationen ausgedacht, z. B. die ,Tame-azons', die Männer zähmen (to tame), und dann die ,Princkazons'. Weil ich als junger Mann klein und etwas schüchtern war, liebte ich die Vorstellung, dass mich große, aggressive Frauen mit physischer Gewalt zum Sex zwingen würden. Dahinter steckt der Wunsch, begehrt zu werden, etwas, das Frauen wie selbstverständlich von Männern erwarten, Männer aber selten umgekehrt bei Frauen erleben. Sex, bei dem die Frau auf dem Bett liegt und man selber obendrauf, ist nicht besonders aufregend. Ich bin ein Mann, ich liebe den Kampf, die Eroberung. Und zufällig liebe ich es besonders, den Kampf zu verlieren und mich der Siegerin zu unterwerfen."

Die Stantoon-Comicbooks, die er seit den 70ern selbst herausgegeben und vertrieben hat, gewähren noch am ehesten Aufschluss über den Mann Eric, weil sie nicht nach Vorgaben entstanden sind. Wrestling – Frau gegen Frau oder Frau gegen Mann – kommt in fast allen von ihnen vor. Selbst die Princkazons nehmen ihre Opfer vor der unvermeidlichen Penetration gerne in die Beingrätsche. In den meisten Kämpfen kommt Erics Lieblingsposition vor, die mal „Queening" oder „Smother Submission", mal „Panty Smother" heißt. Das bedeutet einfach, dass eine Frau im Höschen auf dem Gesicht eines Mannes sitzt, ihm mit ihrer Scham Mund und Nase zudrückt und ihn zwingt, sie zu befriedigen.

Als Eric 1971 seine zukünftige Frau Britt kennenlernte, war er so hingerissen („Du siehst aus, als wärst du einem meiner Comics entsprungen!"), dass er seine sexuelle Unterwerfung öffentlich machte. Ein Kurzfilm und die dazugehörigen Standfotos zeigen, wie das junge Model aus Norwegen den sonst so schüchternen Künstler zu Boden ringt und sich dann triumphierend auf sein Gesicht setzt. Seine Kapitulation war nicht nur symbolisch: Britt blieb seine persönliche Göttin oder sein Dämon und bereitete ihm nach ihrem Gutdünken Lust oder Schmerz. Eric liebte sie mit einer Inbrunst, zu der nur ein Stanton-Charakter fähig ist.

In den letzten Jahren vor seinem Tod am 17. März 1999 hat Eric seine junge Tochter darin unterrichtet, Comics in seinem Stil zu zeichnen. Der hübsche Teenager zeigte ein besonderes Talent für Szenen weiblicher Dominanz, aber die Grausamkeit von Mädchen in diesem Alter ist ja hinlänglich bekannt. Eric lachte dann leise in sich hinein: „Ganz ihre Mutter."

Eric behauptete stets, dass es ihm nichts mehr ausmache, wenn in der Öffentlichkeit Gerüchte über ihn kursierten. Allein das Gerücht, er sei längst tot, ärgerte ihn, weil die Leute deswegen glaubten, sie könnten ungestraft seine Arbeit stehlen. Er hatte seine Illustrationen schon auf Duschvorhängen, Briefpapier und sogar auf Tapeten entdeckt. Und da war dieser Kerl in England, der seine Werke „gesampelt" hatte und damit so reich geworden war, dass Stanton es sich nicht leisten konnte, ihn zu verklagen ...

Dennoch konnte Stanton zuletzt auf ein langes und erfülltes Leben zurückblicken. Nur einen Wunsch hatte er noch vor seinem Tod: Er hätte zu gerne den ultimativen Stanton-Millennium-Kalender produziert. Das klingt nach einem bescheidenen Wunsch für Eric den Wilden, aber er passt perfekt zu dem freundlichen, korrekten Ernest Stanzone, dem kleinen Jungen aus Brooklyn, der es zum König der Fetisch-Welt gebracht hat.

Dian Hanson, Chefredakteurin, LEG SHOW Magazine

LE ROI DU FÉTICHISME

J'ai décroché mon premier job dans l'industrie du sexe en 1976. Par rapport aux critères du secteur, c'était un poste plutôt « soft » : assistante de rédaction dans une prétentieuse revue pornographique appelée Puritan. Ceci dit, c'était déjà assez pour moi. Chaque jour, le courrier apportait son lot de témoignages, de photos, de nouvelles et de publications bizarroïdes que je devais éplucher. Un jour, on m'envoya une étrange petite bande dessinée intitulée The Punished Publisher (L'éditeur châtié), qui annonçait fièrement en couverture « quatre-vingt-une illustrations signées Stanton ». J'étais une fan des dessinateurs underground R. Crumb et S. Clay Wilson et pensais alors avoir déjà vu tous les degrés de perversité. Pourtant, ce Stanton m'ouvrait des horizons dont je n'aurais jamais osé rêver. Les amazones de Crumb étaient systématiquement terrassées par les différentes versions de son double, alors que celles de Stanton tannaient le cuir des mâles. Dans The Punished Publisher, les beautés voluptueuses parvenaient à déjouer les ruses de leur employeur abusif, le maîtrisaient puis le forçaient à sucer un godemiché attaché à leur ceinture. Pour la pauvre petite employée que j'étais, quel pied ! En 1976, le féminisme commençait à fourbir ses premières armes mais peu d'hommes dans mon entourage le prenaient au sérieux. Stanton, lui, non seulement reconnaissait la lutte des femmes, mais comprenait que les hommes pouvaient être émoustillés par ces viragos en colère et nourrir un désir coupable de redresser les torts de leur sexe en se soumettant à leur pouvoir.

A leur pouvoir sexuel, bien entendu. Pour le jeune fantassin féministe que j'étais, dominer sexuellement les hommes était une perspective très séduisante. Je classai donc Stanton dans cette catégorie que nous appelions « les hommes féministes » et ajoutai The Punished Publisher à ma collection privée. Au moment où j'écris ceci, le livre se trouve sur mon bureau et, à l'âge de quarante-six ans, j'ai autant de plaisir à le relire que quand j'en avais vingt-quatre. Sauf qu'aujourd'hui, ce n'est qu'un superbe fantasme de domination et non plus un pamphlet politique. Eric Stanton était un visionnaire mais, même jeune homme, la seule politique qui l'intéressait était celle du sexe.

On raconte que Stanton, né Ernest Stanzone, a eu une jeunesse dissolue. La partie que je préfère de son histoire, vraie ou fausse, est celle où il est lanceur de couteaux. Il est vrai qu'il a grandi à Brooklyn, tout près du vaste parc d'attractions miteux de Coney Island, mais cela n'explique pas qu'un jeune homme timide se retrouve à faire un tel métier ! Etait-il doué ? Sur quoi ou sur qui lançait-il ses couteaux ? Je suppose qu'à cette époque, la vie de foire était encore plus intrépide qu'aujourd'hui. En 1984, j'ai été abordée dans une rue de New York par un certain Paul qui prétendait recruter des femmes pour lutter entre elles dans les vidéos d'Eric Stanton. Je me suis mise à rire, non seulement parce que je connaissais Stanton et que je pouvais imaginer la tête des autres femmes qu'il abordait, mais également parce que je ne comprenais pas pourquoi un artiste aussi talentueux perdrait son temps à produire des vidéos de catch féminin. Une de mes amies fut accostée par ce même homme. Ancienne actrice de porno sans travail et sans peur, elle le suivit dans un bel appartement des quartiers chics où, effectivement, on la fit lutter contre une autre femme. Stanton n'était pas présent mais, six mois plus tard, le fameux Paul contacta le bureau du magazine minable pour lequel je travaillais et demanda à passer une annonce pour une collection de vidéos d'Eric Stanton. Et là, sur ses brochures, je vis mon amie Suzy assise sur le visage d'une autre femme. Quand j'ai demandé à Paul pourquoi le grand Eric Stanton faisait des vidéos de catch, il m'a répondu : « Parce qu'il aime ça ». De toute évidence, c'était là une motivation suffisante pour ce libertin de M. Stanton.

Lorsque j'ai enfin rencontré Eric Stanton pour la première fois en 1991, il avait une bonne soixantaine d'années. Je l'ai trouvé charmant et effacé, même s'il portait toujours la barbichette et ses cheveux noirs coupés à la diable, comme son alter ego de bande dessinée Dastardly. On l'a souvent décrit comme un reclus, mais cela connote un être malsain et insociable qui ne correspond pas à l'homme que j'ai connu. C'était simplement un père de famille qui travaillait tranquillement chez lui, réalisant sans discontinuer ses illustrations et ses Stantoons, de petites bandes dessinées qu'il produisait lui-même pour une clientèle éparpillée dans le monde entier. C'est sans doute la nature provocante de son art qui incite les gens à lui chercher toutes sortes de pathologies mentales. Toutefois, dans son cas, l'art n'est pas nécessairement une fenêtre sur l'âme.

Stanton travailla comme illustrateur fétichiste plus de 50 ans. Quatre-vingt-dix pour cent de son travail était réalisé sur commande. Du fait de son don unique pour adopter, pénétrer, comprendre et apprécier les fantasmes des autres, chacune de ses peintures, de ses illustrations ou de ses planches de bande dessinée fait preuve d'une même passion créative. Cela explique sans doute les nombreuses spéculations contradictoires sur ses penchants sexuels. On sait qu'à ses débuts, il s'est beaucoup inspiré de John Willy, dont il a réalisé des imitations parfaitement crédibles pour Irving Klaw. Si on se base sur ce travail, on en déduit qu'il adorait le bondage et les situations où la femme est soumise. Il a également fait des croquis sophistiqués de talons aiguilles, à la John Willy. On se dit que des dessins aussi brillants ne peuvent avoir surgi que de l'esprit d'un obsédé par la torture du pied. Ensuite, il y a toutes ces bandes dessinées de travestissement pour Female Mimics et d'autres revues américaines de travestis du milieu des années 60 et du début des années 70. Et que penser des puissantes et très troublantes Princkazones, des femmes de deux mètres, avec leurs seins comme des potirons et leurs phallus de bélier ? Ces hybrides homme/femme adorent maîtriser des hommes inférieurs et les forcent à se soumettre à leurs « princks » démesurés. Lorsque j'ai interrogé Eric à se sujet, il a haussé les épaules : « C'était un client qui en a eu l'idée et ça m'a amusé. Une fois que j'ai eu développé les personnages, je les ai incorporés à mes Stantoons. Je me suis rendu compte que quand un client a un fantasme, celui-ci est généralement partagé par beaucoup d'autres. Ils se vendent bien. »

Mais d'où vient le mot « princk » ?

« Comme il s'agissait de femmes avec une bitte ("prick" en anglais), j'ai voulu créer un mot spécial pour leur pénis. J'y ai rajouté un "n" pour que ça sonne plus féminin. Comme "pink". C'est aussi simple que ça. »

En traduisant ainsi toutes les permutations de la perversion, Eric Stanton cachait son jeu autant qu'il le dévoilait. Ses propres fantasmes sont là, exprimés modestement, sans ostentation, sans faire passer ses obsessions personnelles avant celles des autres. C'était son choix. Toutefois, il suffisait de le pousser un peu pour qu'il se confie.

« J'ai toujours aimé les amazones. Le mot seul suffit à m'exciter. J'en ai inventé des variantes, comme les Tame-azones qui dressent les hommes, (du mot Tame, "dompter" en anglais) et les Princkazones. Quand j'étais jeune, j'étais petit et timide, aussi j'adorais l'idée d'être maîtrisé et violé par de grandes femmes agressives. Cela vient de l'envie d'être désiré, une envie que l'on considère naturelle chez la femme mais qu'on attend rarement de l'homme. Le sexe facile, où la femme se couche sur le lit et l'homme lui grimpe dessus, ne m'intéresse pas beaucoup. Je suis un homme, j'aime me battre, j'aime la conquête. La seule différence, c'est que j'aime perdre et être forcé de satisfaire celle qui m'a vaincue. »

Ce sont dans les Stantoons, des bandes dessinées que Stanton publia et commercialisa lui-même à partir des années 70, que l'on apprend à mieux le connaître, car beaucoup n'ont pas été réalisées sur commande. La lutte, entre femmes ou femme contre homme, y est presque omniprésente. Même les Princkazones aiment étouffer leurs victimes entre leurs cuisses avant l'inévitable pénétration. La plupart des combats incluent la position favorite d'Eric, qu'il appelle tantôt Queening, « soumission par étranglement », ou « l'étouffement de la petite culotte » : la femme est assise sur le visage de l'homme couché sur le dos, ses parties intimes protégées par une petite culotte lui écrasant le nez et la bouche. Il n'a pas d'autre choix que de la satisfaire. Lorsqu'Eric rencontra sa future épouse Britt en 1971, ce fut le coup de foudre. (« Vous semblez tout droit sortie de l'une de mes bandes dessinées. ») Il enregistra aussitôt sa soumission à son pouvoir érotique par un petit court métrage et une série de diapos : on y voit le jeune mannequin norvégien luttant contre l'artiste et s'asseyant triomphalement sur son visage. Cette reddition n'était pas purement symbolique. Britt resta toujours sa déesse et son démon, administrant plaisir et douleur selon son gré. Eric l'aima avec toute la ferveur dont seul un personnage de Stanton est capable. Au cours de ses dernières années – il devait mourir le 17 mars 1999 – Eric apprit à sa fille à dessiner des bandes dessinées dans son style. La jolie jeune fille excellait tout particulièrement dans les scènes de domination féminine, mais la cruauté des adolescentes n'est plus à prouver ! Cela faisait sourire fièrement son père : « C'est le portrait craché de sa mère ! » Stanton affirmait qu'après toutes ces années, il n'était plus agacé par les fantasmes que le public projetait sur sa vie, sauf quand on faisait courir le bruit qu'il était déjà mort car, selon lui, certains en profitaient pour lui voler ses œuvres en toute impunité. Il retrouvait ses images, signées par d'autres, sur des rideaux de douche, du papier à lettre et même des papiers peints. Et puis, il y avait l'éternel grief dû à cet homme vivant en Angleterre, devenu tellement riche et célèbre en « copiant » son travail que Stanton n'eut même pas les moyens de le poursuivre en justice... Quoi qu'il en soit, Eric Stanton a eu une vie longue et heureuse. Il ne lui restait plus qu'un objectif à atteindre, m'avait-il dit, peu de temps avant sa mort : il désirait réaliser un calendrier pour l'an 2000. Cela peut paraître une ambition modeste pour ce dévergondé d'Eric Stanton, mais parfaitement en accord avec Ernest Stanzone, ce gentil garçon de Brooklyn appelé à devenir le roi du fétichisme.

Dian Hanson, rédactrice en chef du magazine LEG SHOW

RASSING!
RONT OF
EY, CAN'T
VE YOU
...OH!
-D-E-R!
..JE...
NOT UNTIL YOU'VE EMPT
YOURSELF OUT DARLING
YOU TO COME INTO THAT
AND MAKE HER PREGNAN
COME YOU BASTARD , C
WHIPPERS
E! STOP, I HAVE HAD
...EYAH! ENOUGH...I
VE MADE YOUR POINT..
THING YOU DAMNED
NLY TAKE THAT
NG OUT OF ME...,.
S-E.....

ED
I WANT
ITCH
. . .
ME!
ALL

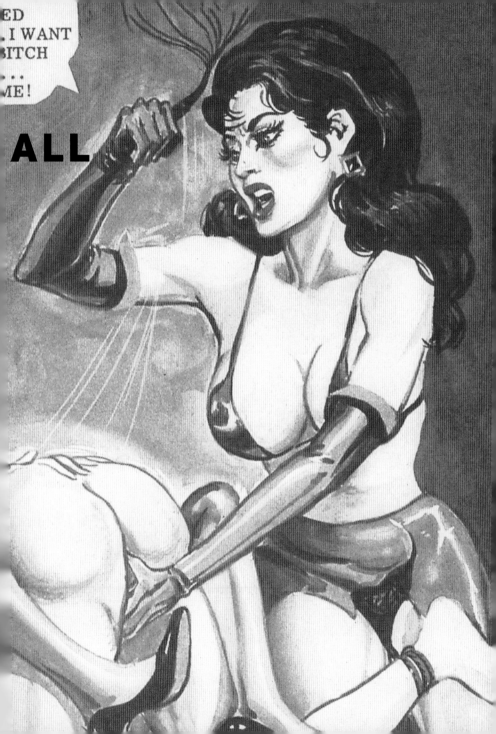

ONCE I GET MY MONEY FROM DIANE WE'LL FLY TO MEXICO FOR THE DEVORCE, TO RENO FOR THE WEDDING... HOW'S THAT HONEY?
OH JEFFRY, I'M SO HAPPY... ARE YOU SURE SHE WON'T TRY TO... NO...
WELL.. THIS IS THE SWEET YOUNG THING YOU'RE SO HEP-PED UP ABOUT? ..PRETTY..
YESS...WE ARE IN A HURRY, ER.. CAN I HAVE MY MONEY?
SORRY, JEFFREY, NO MONEY AND..NO DEVORCE AND THAT IS FINAL...
FINAL MY FOOT! I WANT WHAT'S DUE ME AND I INTEND TO GET IT IF I HAVE TO KILL YOU..UNDER-STAND?
JEFFREY, DON'T GET UPSET... I I'D LIKE TO ... LEAVE, JEFF!

WE'LL LEAVE WHEN I I'M GOOD AND READY AND NOT BEFORE... I SHOULD HAVE KNOWN..YOU'D PULL A STUNT LIKE THIS....
JEFF ... STOP IT! THIS WILL GET US NO.. OH!... LOOK OUT SHE, SHE HAS....

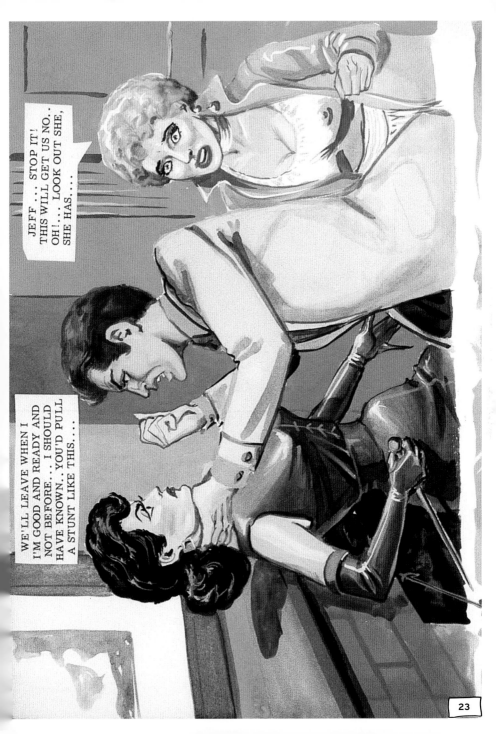

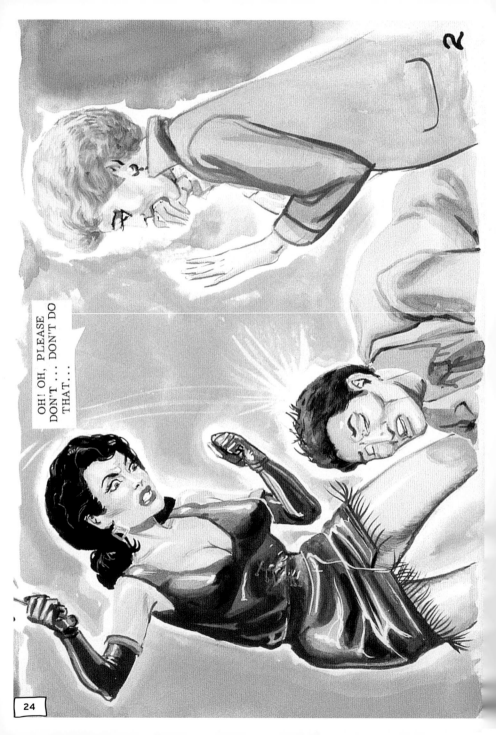

OH! OH, PLEASE DON'T... DON'T DO THAT...

24

2

STOP IT, STOP IT!
TAKE YOUR FILTHY HANDS OFF ME...IF YOU DON'T WANT SOME OF THE SAME...
OH, PLEASE..PLEASE I BEG YOU... DON'T KILL HIM...WE'LL LEAVE RIGHT NOW AND NEVER BOTHER YOU...PLEASE!
I DON'T WANT EITHER OF YOU TO LEAVE.... I NEVER INTENDED TO GIVE MY DARLING UP TO YOU OR ANYONE....
SOB...ISN'T THERE SOME OTHER WAY... I CAN GET SOB .. YOU TO STOP....
NO WAY...HONEY! NO.. WAY.. AT ..ALL! WHAT WAS THAT YOU SAID JEFF? I DIDN'T QUITE GET THAT!
AGHHH!

JUST A-MINUTE MISS,, HONEY ER WHAT EVER YOU CALL YOUR SELF... I'M NOT .. THROUGH WITH YOU BY A LONG SHOT... I'VE MADE SOME PLANS AND THEY INCLUDE YOU... NOW TAKE HOLD OF YOUR PRECIOUS DARLING AND DRAG HIS ASS UPSTAIRS.. WE ARE GOING TO TEACH HIM A LESSON EVEN IF IT KILLS HIM.. OR YOU!
OW! I.. DON'T.. I CAN'T...
CAN'T YOU HELP ME ,(PUFF) HE IS A DEAD WEIGHT... HOW CAN YOU BE SO....
KEEP STILL IF YOU DON'T WANT TO TAKE HIS PLACE DO AS YOU ARE TOLD.... TAKE HIS CLOTHES OFF AND THROW HIS ASS UP ON THE BED...
4

IF YOU DON'T STOP YOUR WHINING AND FINISH TYING HIM UP I'LL MAKE SURE HE'S OF NO USE TO YOU OR ANYONE EVER...
PLEASE DON'T .. I I'LL DO IT ONLY DON'T HURT HIM ANY MORE! OH, DARLING , I LOVE YOU SO....

I WON'T HURT HIM ANYMORE IF YOU WILL.... HIT HIM.... BREAK THE CANE OVER HIS BACK! HIT HIM OR SO HELP ME... YOU'LL WISH YOU HAD...DAMN YOU... LAY IT ON HIM...
HIT HER, HONEY! HIT..ER.. WHAT THE HELL ARE YOU WAITING FOR?
EEEEKKKK!

DIANE... HAVE YOU GONE GONE.. CRAZY?... YOU'VE HAD YOUR FUN NOW... ER UNTIE ME! HONEY ARE YOU ALL RIGHT? IF SHE'S HURT...I'LL GET YOU!!
OH, MY GOD... I THINK ... I THINK I'M BLEEDING!
GET UP! GET UP! YOU'RE NOT HURT! NOT YET THAT IS.. YOU LOVE HIM SO MUCH... WHY! IS HE GOOD IN BED? SHOW ME HOW THE TWO OF YOU MAKE IT! GETIN BED WITH HIM.... NOW!

NOW I MUST SAY THAT IS A PRETTY SIGHT! I DON'T KNOW WHICH OF YOU HAS THE MORE INVITING REAR....HANG ON TIGHT, HONEY! YOU ARE ABOUT TO RIDE YOUR DARLING LIKE YOU'VE NEVER RIDDEN HIM BEFORE!
DON'T MISS HIM... HIM...PLEASE!
GET THE HELL OFF ME... OW...YOUR FOOT... GET YOUR FOOT...YOU..DAMN YOU TOO... YOU ARE HURT HURTING ME... THERE!

WHAT...WHAT ARE YOU DOING BACK THERE? YOU'RE NOT...REALLY HURTING HIM ARE YOU? PLEASE DON'T...HE IS SO GOOD..SO VERY...
HE'S GOOD AND TIGHT! DAMN YOU JEFF, LOOSEN UP...THIS IS GOING IN IF I HAVE RIP YOU APART....OPEN...UP!
UHHH! DON'T DON'T, DIANE.. YOU'LL BUST A BLADDER..EE EEEAYAHHH!
JUST A LITTLE BIT MORE YOU BASTARD.......THERE THAT's BETTER. I KNEW YOU WOULD, PET, YOU ALWAYS WERE SO OBLIGING!

THIS.. THIS IS SO EMBARRASSING! E NEVER DONE THIS IN FRONT OF YONE BEFORE... JEFFREY, CAN'T OU REASON WITH HER? HAVE YOU NO RESPECT FOR ME? oooh... OH! HARDER.... HARDER, H-A-R-D-E-R! I... OH... I LOVE.... YOU... JE...
DIANE! DIANE! STOP, I HAVE HAD ENOUGH OF ...EYAH! ENOUGH...I SAID... YOU'VE MADE YOUR POINT.. I'LL DO ANYTHING YOU DAMNED ...SAY... ONLY TAKE THAT THAT... THING OUT OF ME.... P-L-E-A-S-E......
NOT UNTIL YOU'VE EMPTYED YOURSELF OUT DARLING...I WANT YOU TO COME INTO THAT BITCH AND MAKE HER PREGNANT... COME YOU BASTARD, COME!
10

THIS IS REALLY TOO MUCH, JEFFREY DEAR! THE TWO OF YOU...SO MUCH IN LOVE...YOU WERE SO WILLING TO DIE FOR EACH OTHER BEFORE...AND NOW...NEITHER OF YOU IS WILLING TO TAKE A STRAPPING FOR THE OTHER...GO AHEAD, STUFF YOUR FACES FULL..FIRST ONE TO QUIT GET''S THE LASHING...WHO WILL IT BE..who WILL it be?

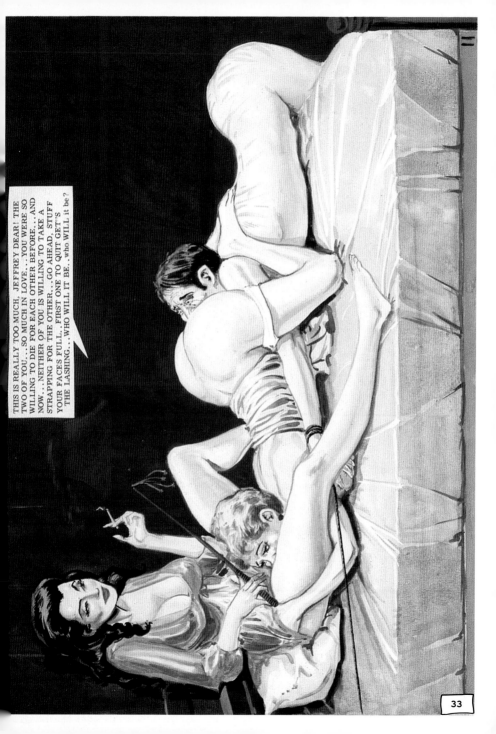

UR WATERFRONT PLACE.
HEY SAID YOU COULDN'T
ET OUT. I THOUGHT I'D
NEVER SEE YOU AGAIN
HAT'S ALL THE NOISE...
THEY...THEY...FOLLOWED
YOU...OH..OH...

BONNIE
& CLARA

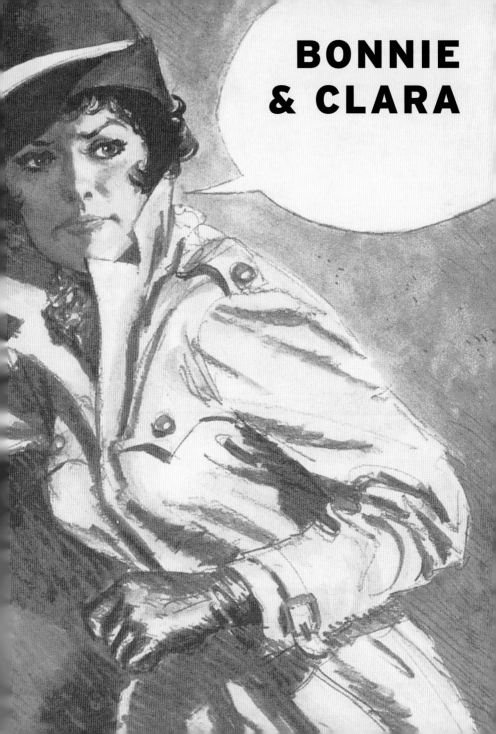

BONNIE and CLARA
WHY DIDN'T YOU LISTEN TO ME, CLYDE? I TOLD YOU YOUR LUCK COULDN'T HOLD. AT LEAST OUR LOOT IS SAFE WITH DOUGLAS. YOU TOLD ME NEVER TRUST LAWYERS BUT WHO ELSE COULD I TURN TO?

'BANG 'BANG
COPS! NOW I KNOW I WAS RIGHT TO TRUST DOUG. THEY WON'T FIND THE MONEY HERE ... BUT... WHAT WILL THEY DO TO ME? OH... CLYDE, I WISH YOU WERE HERE...
KNOCK! KNOCK!
OPEN UP! DAMNIT. IT'S ME, CLARA. HURRY UP... MOVE YOUR ASS BONNIE. THE LAW IS HUNTING EVERYWHERE FOR ME! MOVE IT... BONNIE!
CLARA? THANK GOODNESS I'VE BEEN SO MIXED UP ABOUT WHAT TO DO EVERYTHING'LL BE ALL-RIGHT NOW... SHE'LL KNOW WHAT TO DO... COMING!

WHAT HAPPENED? THE RADIO SAID YOU WERE PINNED DOWN AT OUR WATERFRONT PLACE. THEY SAID YOU COULDN'T GET OUT. I THOUGHT I'D NEVER SEE YOU AGAIN WHAT'S ALL THE NOISE... THEY... THEY... FOLLOWED YOU... OH.. OH...
NOBODY PINS ME DOWN... BY THE TIME THEY GOT UP THE NERVE TO BREAK IN... I WAS GONE... ...THROUGH THE TRAP DOOR IN THE CLOSET FLOOR... I'M HERE THAT'S ALL... COMMOTION DOWNSTAIRS?.. I DON'T KNOW... BUT I WAS NOT FOLLOWED...

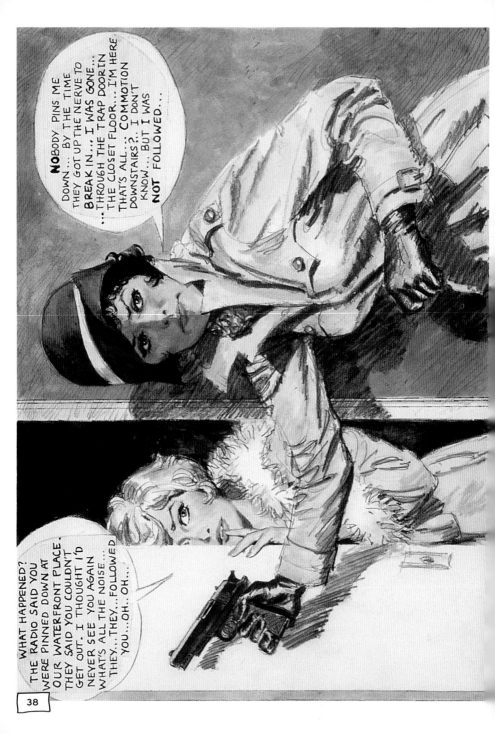

STOW IT! BONNIE, WE'VE GOT TO LAY LOW FOR A WHILE. NO NEED TO WORRY WITH THAT $400,000 YOUR SITTING ON, WE CAN AFFORD TO LIVE REAL WELL JUST BABY AND ME...

I... I DIDN'T KNOW YOU'D BE BACK. YESTERDAY WHEN I HEARD HOW BADLY THE NORTHFIELD BANKJOB WENT, I GAVE THE MONEY, ALL OF IT TO DOUGLAS. YOU KNOW HIM, THE LAWYER. HE SAID IT WOULD BE SAFER WITH HIM...
I KNOW THE BASTARD ALL RIGHT HE PULLED THAT STUNT ON PRETTY FACE SHULTZ.. ..THEN HE SET HIM UP FOR AN AMBUSH... IT WAS PROBABLY HIM WHO FINGERED US FOR NORTHFIELD!

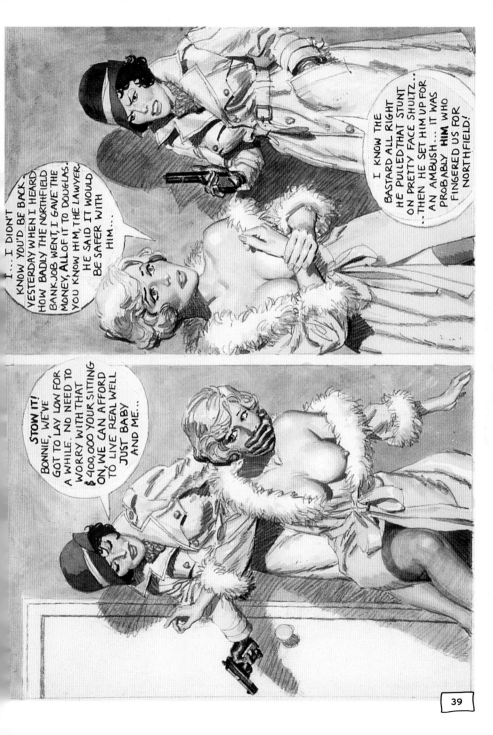

OH ... I'VE DONE IT HAVEN'T I? I'VE... RUINED EVERYTHING... I ALWAYS MAKE THE WRONG DECISION. IF IT WASN'T FOR ME, CLYDE'D PROBABLY STILL BE FREE. WE'LL NEVER GET THE MONEY BACK FROM DOUGLAS... I... KNOW IT... I JUST KNOW IT... CLARA, WILL WE GET THE MONEY? WILL DOUGLAS... GIVE IT BACK?
MAYBE!.. AS GREEDY AS YOUR LAWYER FRIEND IS, I THINK WE CAN MAKE HIM TAKE A FEW WRONG STEPS... ALL WE HAVE TO DO IS GET HIM **HERE**... AWAY FROM HIS FRIEND... AND **WORK** ON HIM. I'VE A FEW PLANS FOR THE SON OF A BITCH...

YOU DON'T DOUBT ME, DO YOU? I'VE ALWAYS TAKEN CARE OF YOU BEFORE! DON'T YOU THINK I KNOW HOW TO HANDLE A BUM LIKE DOUGLAS... WELL ...**DO** YOU?
I... I KNOW YOU'RE CAPABLE OF LOTS... I **KNOW** THAT... BUT DOUGLAS... HE HAS FRIENDS ALL OVER THE CITY... INFLUENTIAL PEOPLE OWE HIM FAVORS HE'LL FIND SOME WAY TO HURT US.
NOT THE WAY I PLAN IT. BESIDES GETTING THE LOOT BACK, WE'RE GOING TO TAKE THAT BIG-SHOT APART.. ..A PIECE AT A TIME. THEN I'M GOING TO SCREW HIM UP SO BAD AND MAKE HIM LOOK SO AWFUL NONE OF HIS FRIENDS'LL WANT TO HELP HIM.

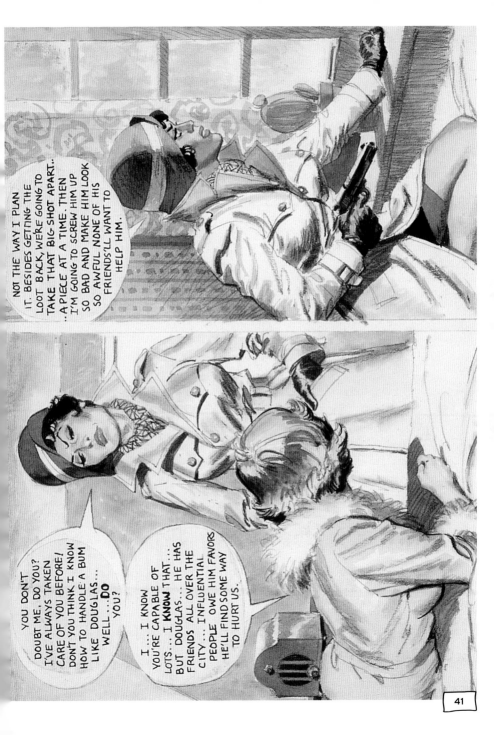

YOU'RE GOING TO DO EXACTLY WHAT I TELL YOU I HELPED YOU THE LAST TIME AND I'LL DO IT NOW, YOU KNOW HOW GOOD IT CAN BE FOR US. NOW WHY DON'T WE JUST RELAX?... WE HAVE BEEN TO... GETHER... ALONE FOR A LONG TIME.
OH CLARA... I'VE THOUGHT ABOUT YOU ALL THE TIME... I WAS WORRIED SOMETHING... WOULD HAPPEN TO KEEP US APART. HOLD ME TIGHT I'M AFRAID OF... BEING SEPARATED AGAIN.

IT WAS NEVER THIS GOOD WITH CLYDE, WAS IT? THERE'S NO MAN WHO CAN PLEASE YOU LIKE I ... THEY DON'T KNOW WHAT A WOMAN FEELS, WHAT SHE REALLY... WANTS... NEEDS... TELL ME, BONNIE, TELL ME HOW GOOD I AM. TELL ME I'M BETTER THAN ANY MAN. YOU KNOW WHAT I WANT TO HEAR YOU SAY.
IT'S TRUE! IT REALLY IS. THERE ISN'T ANY MAN IN THE WORLD WHO COULD MAKE ME FEEL AS GOOD AS YOU DO ALL THEY WANT IS FOR THEIR **OWN** PLEASURE,... BUT YOUR NOT LIKE THAT I LOVE EVERYTHING YOU DO TO ME... I LOVE EVERY... THING I LOVE... YOU!

OH... BABE IT FEELS SO WONDERFUL TO HAVE MY LIPS AGAINST YOUR SKIN. I WANT TO KISS YOU EVERYWHERE I WANT TO TASTE YOU AND LICK YOU AND FEEL OUR NAKED BREASTS RUBBING TO... GETHER...
I WILL, BONNIE, I WILL BUT FIRST WE HAVE TO SETTLE SOMETHINGS ABOUT DOUGLAS JUST A FEW THINGS. I WON'T TAKE ANY TIME AT ALL. THEN WE'LL HAVE OUR FUN.
I WANT IT TOO. DON'T WAIT TOO LONG. I'M SO HOT AND WET, ALL YOU'LL HAVE TO DO IS TOUCH ME AND I'LL BLOW UP, BUT I KNOW YOU'LL MAKE IT LAST. YOU KEEP ON EDGE FOR SO LONG...

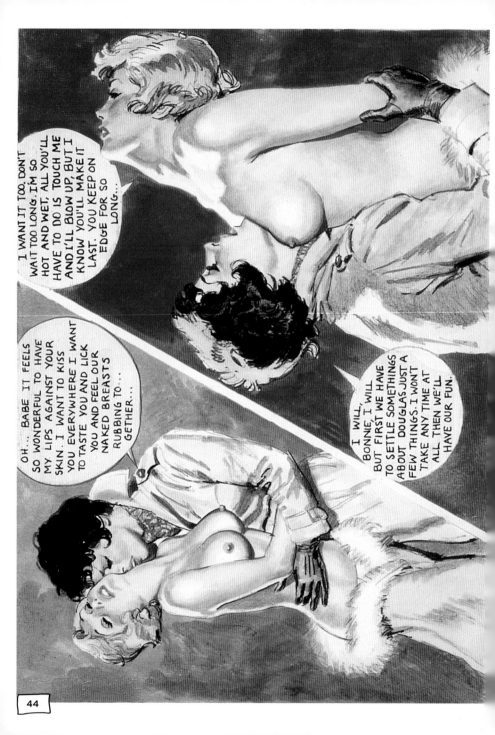

OW!... WHAT THE HELL WAS THAT FOR? DON'T YOU REALIZE WE HAVE TO DO SOMETHING TO HIM TOO.
I WON'T PUT UP WITH BEING USED. YOU JUST WANT MONEY SAME AS DOUGLAS. HE THOUGHT HE WAS A BIG MAN JUST BECAUSE I LET HIM...
SLAP!
YOU LET HIM WHAT? I'M AWAY FROM YOU FOR A LOUSY MONTH AND YOU TURN INTO A SLUT. HOW COULD YOU JUMP INTO THE SACK WITH A CREEP LIKE HIM? YOU LITTLE BITCH.. I...
I'M SORRY I WAS ALONE. I NEEDED SOME-ONE TO TELL ME WHAT TO DO... PLEASE... (CHOKE)...

YOU ALWAYS USH ME BONNIE. YOU ALWAYS PULL SOME FOOL STUNT AND GET ME MAD. I OUGHT TO BEAT YOUR BLOODY ASS!
DON'T HURT ME. I DIDN'T WANT TO.. D.. DOUGLAS.. HE FORCED ME!
LIKE HELL HE DID. I KNOW YOU BETTER THAN THAT. THINK OF THIS NEXT TIME YOU WANT TO TURN TRAMP!
MY HAND! YOU'LL BREAK MY FINGERS. STOP...HURTING... ME ... I WON'T DO IT AGAIN! STOP...

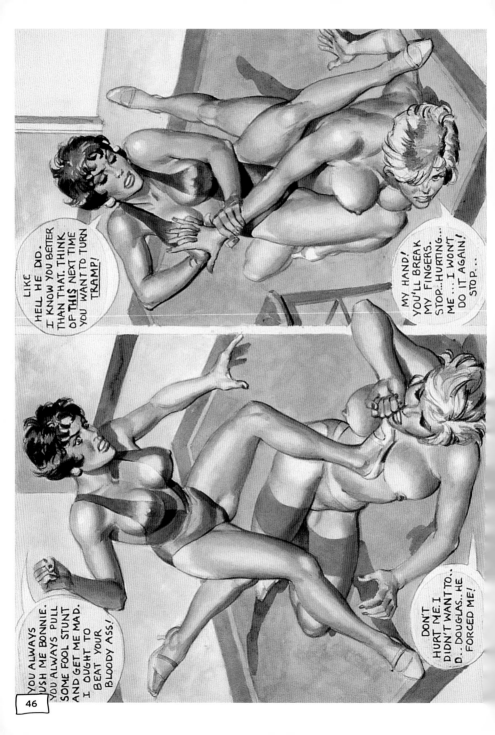

DAMN RIGHT YOU WON'T AND YOU'LL DO EXACTLY AS I SAY! YOU'RE GOING TO SOFTEN DOUGLAS UP, AND THEN I'LL CRUSH HIM... AND REMEMBER, I..[CRACK] MAKE [CRACK] THE [CRACK] RULES!

HOW COULD YOU STAND DOUGLAS' WEAK HAND ON YOU WHEN YOU'VE FELT MY STRONG FINGERS DIG INTO YOUR TITS LIKE THIS, TELL ME YOU DON'T LIKE THIS!
DON'T! YOUR HURTING ME PLEASE... CLARA... CLARA! OHH, CLARA, YES I ... I'D FORGOTTEN WHAT IT'S LIKE TO BE WITH SOMEONE WHO MAKES ME DO WHAT I SHOULD.

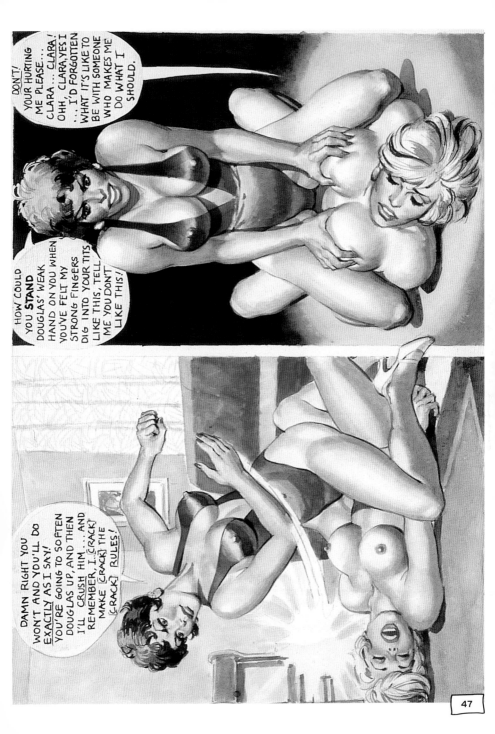

THIS IS IT. YOU'RE WHERE YOU BELONG, BONNIE. I'M GOING TO KEEP YOU HERE UNTIL YOU'VE LEARNED TO BEHAVE.
THAT'S IT!.. THAT'S... IT! OHH... YES! USE YOUR... ...MOUTH!... ...YOUR NOSE... SUCK!..BLOW! OHH..... DAMN YOU!
MMPH... YES MAKE ME DO IT...OHH... CLARA...(MUFFLE) I LOVE... BEING FORCED..

THE NEXT DAY IN DOUG HARDEN'S OFFICE, THE SLICK LAWYER IS IMPLEMENTING PLANS OF HIS OWN.
YOU KNOW, BONNIE, IT WAS SMART OF YOU TO PUT THE MONEY IN MY HANDS. I'LL MAKE IT WORK FOR YOU AND WE'LL BOTH ENJOY, THE PROFITS, OF COURSE, IT'LL BE TIED UP FOR AWHILE. I'M SURE YOU UNDERSTAND...
CERTAINLY, DEAREST. AFTER ALL, YOU'RE THE ONE WITH THE BRAINS. I'LL DO WHATEVER YOU SAY. I TRUST YOU COMPLETELY. I'VE ALWAYS NEEDED SOMEONE TO TAKE CARE OF ME.
IT MAKES ME VERY HAPPY TO HEAR YOU SAY THAT. I ONLY HOPE THAT THE TRUST YOU FEEL FOR ME CAN GROW INTO SOMETHING MUCH MORE MEANINGFUL!
WHY, DOUGLAS, THIS IS ALL SO... SUDDEN,.. YOU MAKE ME.. OH FEEL LIKE A HELPLESS LITTLE GIRL, YOUR SO STRONG SO... COMMANDING.

THAT EVENING... AT THE RITZ.
YOU LOOK BEAUTIFUL. I'M TEMPTED TO LOCK YOU UP WHERE NO OTHER MAN CAN SEE YOU.
AND WHAT WOULD YOU DO TO ME THEN? PUT ME IN SOME SORT OF BONDAGE?
... AND THEN I WRAPPED UP THE ROWES-BURG CASE, I WAS MASTERFUL THE JUDGE PERSONALLY CONGRADULATED ME. CALLED ME BRILLIANT
WHY EVEN IN COLLEGE I WAS RECOGNIZED AS A GENIUS. THE OTHER FELLOWS PRACTICALLY BEGGED ME TO HELP THEM OUT. I TOLD THEM THAT IF THEY DIDN'T DO IT THEMSELVES, THEY'D GAIN NOTHING FROM IT.
YOU KNOW, I'LL BET YOU'VE NEVER GOTTEN YOURSELF INTO A SITUATION YOU COULDN'T CONTROL I CAN'T IMAGINE WHAT IT WOULD TAKE TO OVERCOME YOU!

YOU GROW LOVLIER AS EVENING PROCEEDS, BONNIE. I INSIST THAT YOU COME UP TO MY APARTMENT FOR A DRINK. I WON'T LET YOU SAY NO. BESIDES I STILL HAVEN'T TOLD YOU ABOUT MY GRADE SCHOOL DAYS.
I WOULDN'T WANT TO MISS **THAT!** I WISH THERE WAS SOMETHING I COULD DO TO ENTERTAIN YOU THIS MUCH. MAYBE I CAN THINK OF SOMETHING, SOME SPECIAL SURPRISE THAT YOU'LL LIKE AS MUCH AS I LIKE YOUR STORIES

IN HIS APARTMENT BONNIE CONTINUES TO PLAY HER PART
OH, DOUG, THESE DRINKS ARE GOING TO MY HEAD, I FEEL SO WARM, I FEEL LIKE DANCING AND SINGING. HOW CAN I THANK YOU FOR THE WONDERFUL TIME YOU'VE SHOWN ME?
YOU DON'T HAVE TO DO ANYTHING SPECIAL BONNIE, JUST RELAX AND LET YOURSELF RESPOND TO ME THE WAY A WOMAN INEVITABLY DOES TO A SUPERIOR MAN. YOU'LL DO EVERYTHING... EVERYTHING... TO PLEASE ME. ISN'T THAT RIGHT?
YES, DOUGLAS, YES, I'M SORRY I DIDN'T DO THOSE SPECIAL THINGS YOU WANTED ME TO DO LAST TIME. I'LL MAKE IT UP TO YOU... NOW!

THERE'S ONLY ONE OTHER THING. I KNOW YOU WERE SPENDING A LOT OF TIME WITH THAT... THAT WOMAN, CLARA. SHE MAY TRY TO GET HER CLAWS INTO YOU AGAIN IT'S IMPORTANT THAT YOU HAVE NOTHING TO DO WITH HER.
BUT SHE'S ALWAYS BEEN MY FRIEND. SHE LOOKS OUT FOR ME. WHEN CLYDE USED TO GET MAD AND SAY I'D BEEN DUMB IT WAS HER WHO STUCK UP FOR ME. I JUST CAN'T FORGET ALL THAT.
NO! I WON'T HAVE YOU THAT WAY. WHATEVER IS MINE IS COMPLETELY MINE. THAT'S THE WAY IT'S GOING TO BE WITH YOU. CLARA WILL ONLY MAKE TROUBLE. TELL ME YOU WON'T SEE HER AGAIN.
PLEASE. DON'T MAKE ME SAY THAT, DON'T... OH, DOUGLAS, YOU'RE SO FORCEFUL! YES, I... I PROMISE. I'LL NEVER SEE CLARA AGAIN! SHE NEVER CARED FOR ME THIS DEEPLY, THIS... --FULLY!

THAT'S WHAT I WANTED TO HEAR. NOW I WILL POSSESS YOU UTTERLY. YOU WILL GIVE YOURSELF TO ME IN EVERYWAY VERY SOON, ALL MEMORIES OF THAT ROTTEN BITCH, WILL LEAVE YOU.
I'VE NEVER MET A MAN LIKE YOU. JUST BEING NEAR YOU HAS GOTTEN ME SO EXCITED. I CAN'T WAIT ANY LONGER... PLEASE MY DEAR, TAKE ME!.. ..NOW! SHOW ME WHAT A REAL MAN CAN DO, MAKE ME A COMPLETE WOMAN.

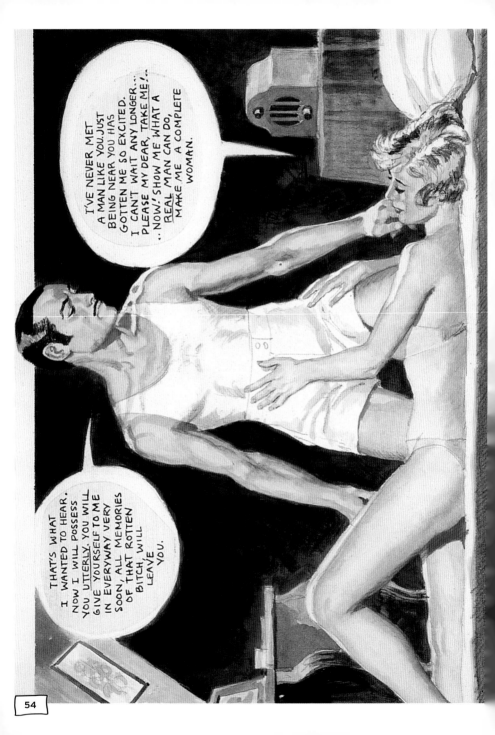

YOU ARE SO LUCKY BONNIE. THERE ARE COUNTLESS WOMEN WHO WOULD BEG TO BE WHERE YOU ARE RIGHT NOW, SHARING THIS MOMENT WITH ME YET I SELECTED YOU. AS WE MAKE LOVE I WANT YOU TO REMEMBER HOW VERY FORTUNATE YOU ARE THAT I'VE DECIDED TO TAKE YOU TONIGHT.
THE WAY YOU LOVE YOURSELF I'M SURPRISED YOU EVEN BOTHER WITH GIRLS. WHY DONT YOU JUST TAKE YOURSELF OUT, THEN COME BACK AND TAKE A MIRROR TO BED.

YOU'VE GOT A LOT OF EXPLAINING TO DO SHYSTER. BONNIE IS MY GIRL AND IT'S MY MONEY YOU TALKED HER OUT OF. THE LAST JOKER WHO TRIED SOME-THING SIMILAR, GOT A BULLET RIGHT BETWEEN HIS... LEGS.

NOW, CLARA, HE'S NO GOOD TO YOU WITH A COUPLE OF BULLETS IN HIM. I'M SURE DOUGLAS WILL STRAIGHTEN THINGS OUT IF YOU ONLY GIVE HIM A CHANCE..ISN'T THAT RIGHT DOUGLAS?
LIKE HELL! I DON'T DEAL WITH SLUTS THE LIKES OF YOU. BONNIE AND THE MONEY ARE MINE!

YOU CREEP! LET ME EXPLAIN SO EVEN AN ASS LIKE YOU CAN UN-DERSTAND WHAT'S BEING SAID... PAY ATTENTION!
DON'T YOU TELL ME TO... ARGH!
YOU'LL DO EXACTLY AS I SAY OR I'LL BUST YOU UP SO BAD YOU WON'T KNOW WHETHER TO WIPE YOUR ASS OR BRUSH YOUR TEETH!
GET OUT OF HERE RIGHT NOW. BONNIE, TELL THIS LUNATIC TO SPLIT!

I OUGHT TO TIE YOUR SHRIVELED THREE PIECE SET TO THE BED FRAME AND PLUCK OUT THAT UGLY MOUSTACHE ONE HAIR AT A TIME. YOU'LL NEVER TOUCH BONNIE OR MAYBE ANYOTHER GIRL AFTER I'VE FINISHED WITH YOU!
CLARA... GET A GRIP ON YOURSELF. IF WE JUST HURT HIM... EVEN IF IT GETS US THE MONEY, HE'LL GET HIS REVENGE IN THE END. REMEMBER WHAT THE PLAN WAS... IT'S THE ONLY WAY!

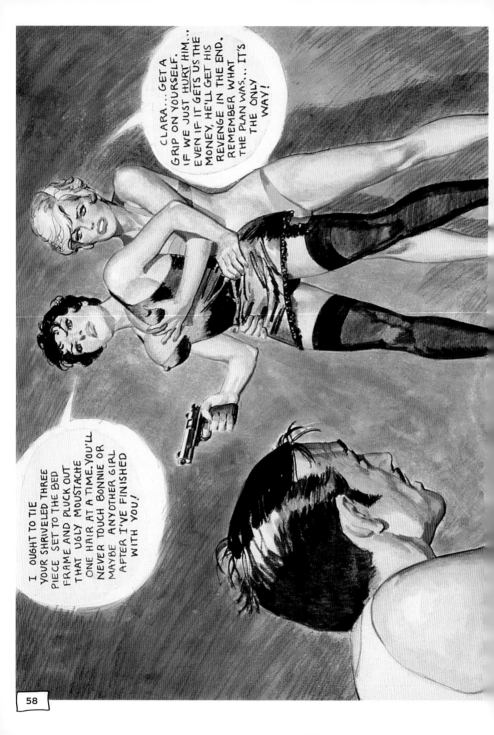

TO BAD WE CAN'T SHOW HIM OFF IN COURT LIKE THIS. THE BEST SIDE UP, MR. DOUGLAS HARDEN.
IT'D BRING BACK PUBLIC FLOG-GING... OR CASTRA-TION.
OW! NOT SO TIGHT DAMN YOU BONNIE HOW COULD YOU DO THIS TO ME!?
YOU MAY THINK YOU CAN BEND ME TO YOUR WILL BUT IT WON'T HAPPEN, I DON'T CARE WHAT YOU TRY, I WON'T PART WITH THE $ 400,000 ... GO AHEAD DO YOUR WORST!

MMM... WHAT PALE SOFT CHEEKS... I WONDER HOW IT'LL STAND UP TO A GOOD LONG SCRATCHING. MY NAILS SINK RIGHT IN... DON'T THEY DOUGLAS?
LET ME LOOSE, YOU TWO FACED BITCH. GET YOUR HANDS OFF ME. OUCH! STOP THAT! DAMN!
HE DESERVES A LOT WORSE THAN GETTING SCRATCHED. LIKE THIS FOR STARTERS. A FEW GOOD, SWIFT KICKS IN THE ASS'LL SOFTEN HIM UP... AND MAYBE ONE OR TWO RIGHT IN THE NUTS.
WAIT A MIN... AEEE YOU CRAZY BITCH!

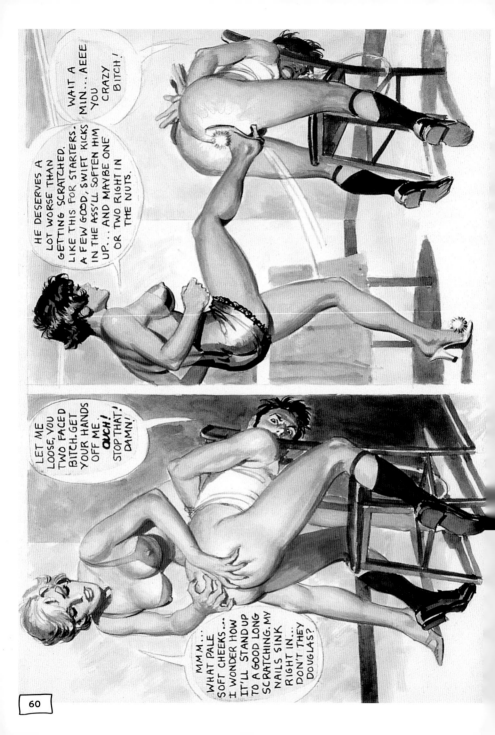

LET'S HEAR YOU... CRY. LET BONNIE SEE WHAT YOU'RE REALLY MADE OF. I JUST WISH YOU COULD GET A LOOK AT HOW PITI- FULLY STUPID YOU LOOK RIGHT NOW...
OW! SOONER OR LATER YOU'LL HAVE TO LET ME GO AND UHH! WHEN YOU DO... I'LL TAKE..AHH! STEPS TO SEE YOU BOTH PAY DEARLY FOR THIS... DAMN!

SHUT YOUR UGLY MOUTH! ...AND DON'T BE SO SURE ABOUT GETTING OUT OF HERE. I'VE KILLED MEN BEFORE, HARDEN. ONE MORE WON'T MEAN ANYTHING!
SLAP

THIS IS WHAT YOU'LL GET IF YOU DON'T COME AROUND PRETTY DAMN QUICK, I COULD PULL THE TRIGGER RIGHT NOW AND BlOW OUT WHAT LITTLE BRAIN YOU HAVE BUT THAT MIGHT SCREW UP OUR GETTING THE CASH. IT'LL GO A LOT SMOOTHER IF YOU JUST SIGN IT BACK OVER TO BONNIE.
THAT'S NOT AS EASY AS IT SOUNDS, THERE'S A LOT OF PAPERWORK INVOLVED I COULDN'T DO IT WITHOUT GOING BACK TO THE OFFICE AND HANDLING THE BOOKS YOU HAVE TO BELIEVE ME.
I THINK YOU CAN THINK OF A QUICKER WAY TO GET THE MONEY TO US WHAT YOU NEED IS SOMETHING TO GET YOUR MIND WORKING... HERE ON THE CENTER OF YOUR PERSONALITY
LISTEN THE SOONER YOU LET ME LOOSE THE SOONER YOU'LL GET THE MONEY IT'S AS SIMPLE AS THAT NOW WHY DON'T YOU WISE UP AND JUST UNTIE ME. YOU'LL HAVE THE MONEY... TOMORROW... WHAT ARE YOU DOING TO MY...

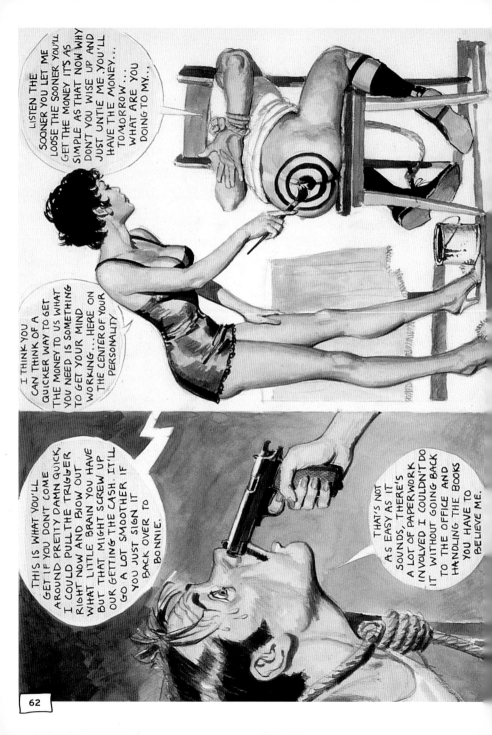

FIRST ROUND, DARLING. IF HE WIGGLES TO MUCH I'LL PUT MY FOOT IN HIS FACE... AND REMEMBER, THE BASTARD'S STILL SITTING ON OUR $ 400,000 SO THROW HARD AND STRAIGHT!
WHA... WHAT ARE YOU TWO DOING BACK THERE? WHAT ARE YOU TALKING ABOUT? IF YOU WANT THE MONEY SOONER I MIGHT BE ABLE TO GET IT TODAY HOW ABOUT THAT? HOW ABOUT IF I GET IT FOR YOU TODAY? WE DON'T HAVE TO PLAY THESE GAMES ANYMORE LET ME GO TO MY OFFICE...
DON'T WORRY I WASN'T SO SURE ABOUT THIS WHEN WE STARTED, BUT NOW I'M WITH YOU ALL THE WAY. I WANT TO HURT HIM SO BAD HE'LL BE AFRAID TO EVEN LOOK MY WAY!

WHAT AN INVITING TARGET, I SAY THE WINNER GETS TO DECIDE WHAT HAPPENS TO HIM NEXT. IF ITS ME, I CAN THINK OF SOMEWHERE ELSE TO STICK ONE OF THESE ... THAT WILL REALLY MAKE HIM COOPERATIVE.
SOUND'S GOOD. IF I WIN, I'M GOING TO TURN THAT CHAIR AROUND, GET CLYDE'S OLD BASEBALL, AND USE DOUGLAS' FACE FOR PITCHING PRACTICE RIGHT NOW LET'S CONCENTRATE ON BULLSEYE THERE.

COMING YOUR WAY MY LOVE . . . LITTLE RED FLYING KISSES FOR YOU ALONE . . . MAY IT GIVE YOU AN EVER LOVING PAIN IN THE ASS.

OOWW!
NO MORE PLEASE! I'LL DO EVERYTHING YOU ASK I DIDN'T INTEND TO KEEP ALL OF THE MONEY, ONLY MY COMMISSION, HONEST I SWEAR!
ANY SYMPATHY I HAD FOR YOU IS GONE... I CAN SEE NOW WHAT A WEAK DIRTY SHIT YOU REALLY ARE, YOU CAN KISS YOUR ASS GOODBYE. I WAS OFF THE MARK BEFORE BUT I'LL PUT A LITTLE MORE SPIN ON THE NEXT ONE AND ZIP IT TO YOU SPECIAL DELIVERY...

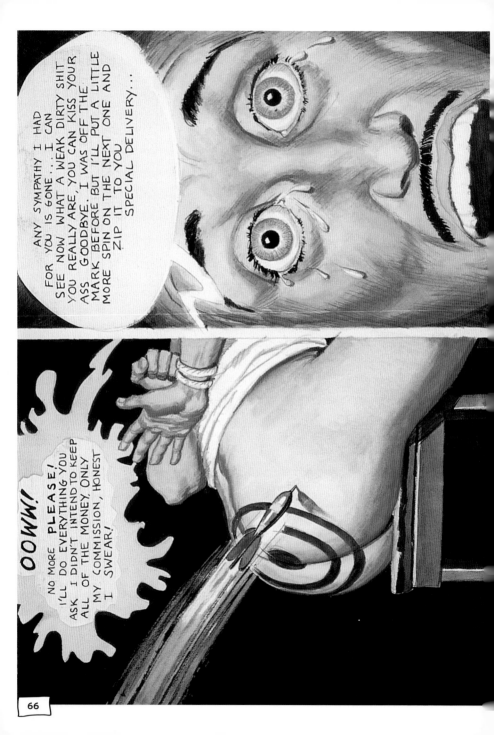

I HOPE IT HURTS LIKE HELL... I REALLY DO. BRACE YOURSELF, DOUGLAS HERE COMES NUMBER THREE!

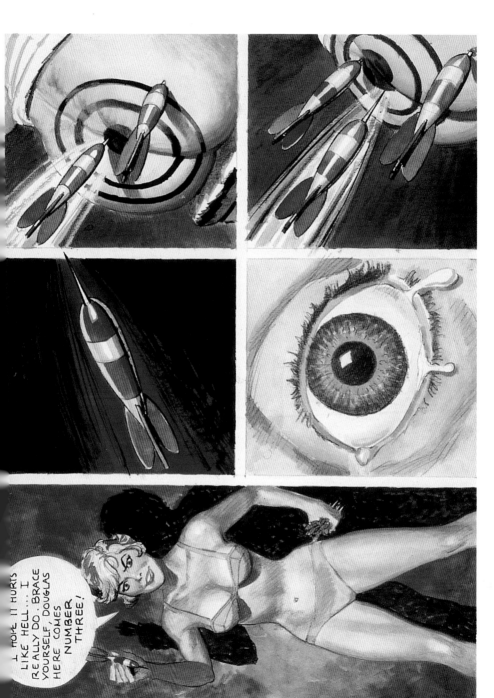

WE SHOULD TRAIN HIM TO LET US SIT ON HIS FACE. THAT'S WHAT I COULD USE NOW, I'M SO HOT!
NAIL HIM BONNIE. I LOVE THE WAY YOUR PUTTING THEM IN AS DEEP AS THEY'LL GO. MAKE THAT LAST ONE COUNT. OOH! I'M GETTING WET JUST WATCHING
DARN! NO BULLSEYES... AND ONLY ONE GOT CLOSE. OH WELL, I GUESS I'LL JUST HAVE TO PRACTICE, PRACTICE PRACTICE, YOU DON'T MIND... DOUGLASS!
FOR MERCY SAKE, TAKE THEM OUT. IT HURTS SO MUCH! I WANT TO SEE A DOCTOR... I COULD DIE OF BLOOD POISON, PLEASE!

LET'S SEE HOW HE LIKES BEING THE ONE WHO GETS SOMETHING STUCK IN HIM. HERE IT COMES... DOUGLAS.
HOLD TIGHT, LAWYER BOY! I'M A LOT BETTER SHOT THAN BONNIE. JUST KEEP THAT ROUND LITTLE ASS STILL FOR ANOTHER SECOND AND YOU'LL FIND OUT WHAT IT FEELS LIKE TO GET BULLSEYED.
NOOO! CLARA! AWOOO! NO MORE!

THAT WAS JUST GREAT. WE SHOULD TAKE HIM OUT TO DINNER... CAN YOU SEE HIM... ...SITTING THERE, ON HIS POOR ASS... AND WHEN HE HAS TO SIT ON THE JOHN... OUCH! HE'S COMPLETELY UNDER OUR CONTROL... LET'S MAKE LOVE NOW SO HE CAN SEE WHO I REALLY CARE FOR!
STOP TALKING CRAZY YOU DAMNED BITCHES. GET ME OUT OF THIS. I'M LOSING TOO MUCH BLOOD. DON'T YOU TWO CARE ABOUT ANYTHING BUT YOUR LOOT AND EACH OTHER? YOU STILL NEED ME FOR THE MONEY... THIS THING ISN'T OVER YET!

DID YOU HEAR WHAT MOUNTAIN MAN SAID... WE BETTER RUN AWAY AND HIDE SOME-WHERE... I'M SHAKING ALL OVER AREN'T YOU, CLARA?
WHEN YOU REMOVE ALL DARTS I'LL GIVE HIM WHAT COMES NEXT... WHEN HE GOES TO COURT AGAIN, HE'LL STAY ON HIS FEET... OF COURSE IF WE DO OUR JOB WELL ENOUGH HE WON'T BE FIT TO EVER TRY ANOTHER CASE!

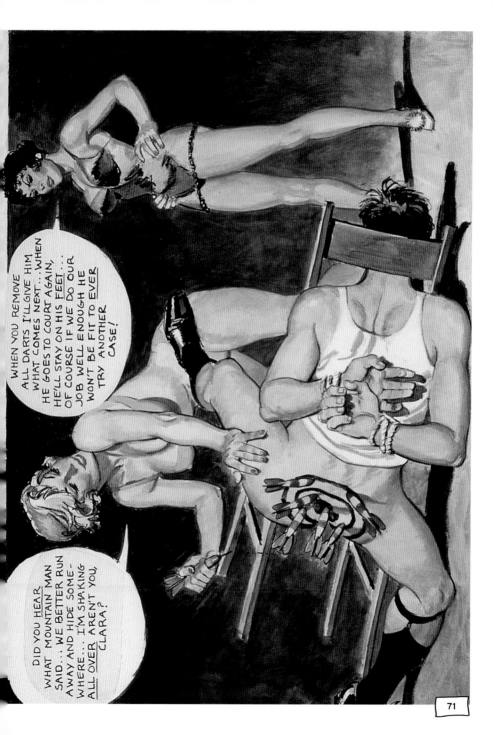

HEAVENS, DOUGLAS, YOUR CHEEKS REALLY DO BEG TO BE ABUSED! I CAN THINK OF A HUNDRED AND ONE WAYS I'D LOVE TO MISTREAT THEM. IT'S JUST AMAZING HOW MANY COLORS COME TO THE SURFACE WITH EACH SUCCEEDING SLAP, HOW'D YOU LIKE A STRAPPING... OR A NICE LONG NECKED WINE BOTTLE?
OOH! DAMN... CLARA, YOU'RE... MAKING... ME SO HOT T-TALKING LIKE THAT. SEEING HIM SIT ON THAT BOTTLE WOULD SURE PAY HIM BACK FOR SOME OF THE AWFUL THINGS HE WANTEDTO DO TO ME.
SON-OF-A BITCHIN... OW! OW! SO HELP ME IF I GET MY HANDS ON YOU, I'LL... OW! BONNIE... PLEASE PLEASE! MAKE HER STOP!

ALLRIGHT, HARD ASS, I'VE FREED YOU... I'M GOING TO PROVE TO BONNIE AND YOU THAT NOT ONLY AM I BETTER THAN YOU IN BED... BUT BETTER THAN YOU AT YOUR OWN GAME. .. GET UP AND FIGHT!
I'LL BEAT YOUR DYKE ASS FOR THIS CUNT...

I'M GOING TO START BY MESSING UP YOUR FACE. URGH!
THANKS FOR THE IDEA, STUPID! I DIDN'T THINK I COULD MAKE YOUR PUSS ANY UGLIER... BUT I'LL HAVE FUN TRYING.

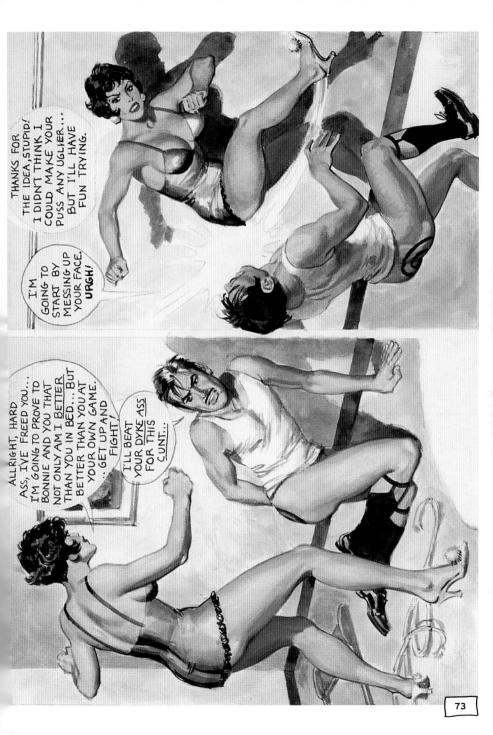

WHAT'S THIS BIG SHOT? YOUR TUMMY IS SOFTER THAN YOUR ASS CHEEKS... SOME TOUGH GUY... CAN'T HOLD HIS OWN AGAINST A MERE GIRL!
ARGH! YOU... YOU CALL YOUR... SELF.... A... OOF!

TELL ME MORE... I WANT TO HEAR HOW YOU'RE GOING TO PUT ME DOWN... PHYSICALLY... YOUR ALL MOUTH... DOUGLAS... DON'T HAVE A MUSCLE TO BACK UP YOUR FANTASY!

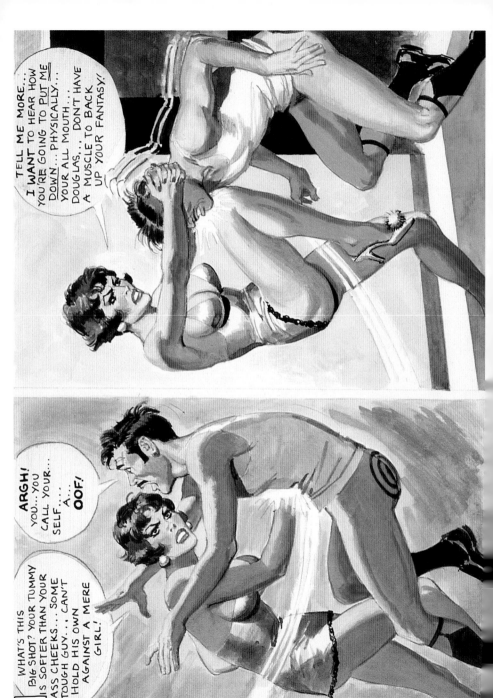

YOUR BEST WEAPON IS YOUR MOUTH, HARD ON, BUT THAT'S ABOUT IT. SHUT IT UP AND YOU HAVE NO OFFENSE. WELL COME ON BIG MAN, COME UP WITH SOMETHING... AND I DIDN'T MEAN YOUR LITTLE DINKY DOO!
BE... BE CAREFUL... YOU... ARE GOING TO 'OKE ME MAH PLIS... IH'VE BEEN FEELING ILL LATELY... YOU...'RE, **OWW!** THAT'S IT... LET'S STOPPFF CAN'F WE TALKK? WOK SOMTIN **OUT!**

YOU'VE GOT SOME BALLS GETTING ... EXCITED WITH ME... ROVER... IF GETTING BEAT UP TURNS YOU ON... I'M ONLY TOO WILLING TO OBLIGE... HOW DO YOU WANT IT, JASPER, BLOODY OR JUST BRUIZES? BRUIZES!
NO... NOO...NO MORE! I GIVE... I'LL GIVE YOU THE MONEY. STOP... MY FACE. DON'T HIT MY FACE ANYMORE. PLEASE!

MMN... I. I WANT TO LET... LOOSE ON YOU! I WANT TO GO ALL OVER YOU... I WANT YOUR FACE TO REWARD ME FOR MY SWEET VICTORY!
LET'S GO... BIG STUFF! .. YOUR HEAD DOWN BETWEEN MY LEGS OR I'LL RIP YOUR DAMNED EARS OFF. YOU'RE SO GOOD AT GETTING YOUR ROCKS OFF WITH GIRLS BUT YOU NEVER GIVE BACK. I'M GOING TO GIVE YOU A LESSON IN HOW TO PLEASE! A FIRST FOR YOU! DOING SOMETHING FOR SOMEBODY OTHER THAN YOURSELF.
OH NO... BONNIE TOLD HER! ... SHE KNOWS HOW MUCH I HATE THAT ... I CAN'T DO THAT ... IT MAKES ME... SICK... I'LL HAVE TO BEG HER .. OHH! NOOO!!

SUCK, YOU FUGGING SHYSTER USE YOUR LIPS. USE YOUR TONGUE. YOU'D BETTER GET GOOD AT THIS FAST, OR IT'S GOING TO BE YOUR LIMP DICK INSTEAD OF CHUBBY ASS THAT GETS USED FOR A DART BOARD NEXT. ... BE AS GOOD AS BONNIE.
YOU'RE SMOTHERING ME!.. PLEASE MY NOSE... DON'T MFFMH DAMN YOU... I CAN'T DO WHAT YOU ASK. SHOW SOME MERCY!
NOTHING WILL STOP HER. I FEEL SO HELPLESS! I CAN'T LET THIS BREAK MY WILL... CAN'T... BREAK ... ME.
YOU SPINELESS SCHMUCK. YOU ARE GOOD FOR SOMETHING OTHER THAN RUNNING YOUR TOOL UP YOUR FIST. OHHH! THAT'S GOOD. KEEP IT UP! I COULD RIDE YOUR FACE ALL DAY... I'M GOING TO POP MY CORK... HARDER, HARDEN! OHHHH!!! YES, YES, YES! OH..OH..
OHHH!
OH.!

MUCH LATER...
DON'T BOTHER COVERING YOURSELF THERE'S NOTHING THERE. NOW GET ON OVER TO THE TABLE AND WRITE A CHECK FOR EVERYTHING YOU TOOK. THEN I HAVE SOME OTHER PAPERS I WANT YOU TO SIGN.
OTHER PAPERS? .... NO!
JUST SIGN, HANDCOCK! UNLESS YOU WANT YOUR HEAD VENTI-LATED?
I KNOW WHAT YOU'RE PLANNING. YOU'RE TRYING TO RUIN ME WELL I HAVE LOTS OF FRIENDS.. IT WON'T TAKE ME LONG TO GET.. GET BACK!

EACH TIME YOU FAIL A CHORE... YOU GET THE LASH! MY SIGNATURE!
I SCRUBBED THE TOILET... CLEANED THE BATHROOM FLOOR. I EVEN HAND LAUNDERED YOUR UNDER-WEAR! YOU'RE ASKING TOO MUCH OF ME!
NO MORE BACKTAIK, LOVE! YOU SASSED YOUR LAST ASS,...
YOW! ENOUGH!
CLACK

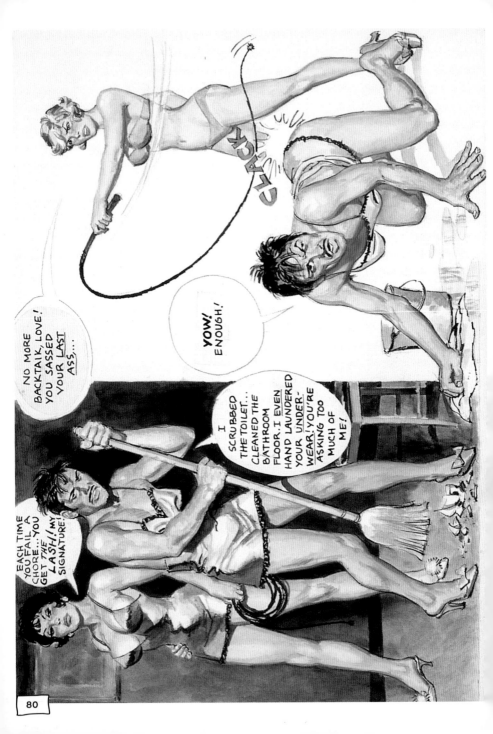

ONE TELLS ME THIS... THE OTHER TELLS ME THAT... I CAN'T DO... NOTHING RIGHT AROUND HERE...
NOW YOU MADE ANOTHER MESS. CLEAN IT UP OR I'LL RUB YOUR FACE IN IT... ... AGAIN
I'M NOT DOING ANY-THING.... ANYMORE?

DO YOU THINK BECAUSE YOU'RE WEARING A SKIRT, I'LL TREAT YOU LIKE A WOMAN.
MY MANHOOD ISN'T COMPLETELY DESTROYED SIMPLY BECAUSE YOU FORCED ME INTO A SKIRT!

THAT'S FOR YOUR MAN-HOOD, DUMPLING... I'LL GIVE YOU A CHANGE OF SEX... PERMANENTLY! SCREW YOU!
UGH! OH... GOD... I THINK YOU BROKE SOMETHING!

YOU FOOLED ME, HARDEN. I REALLY THOUGHT WE HAD YOU WITH THE WINE BOTTLE BIT... OR WHEN WE TOOK TURNS SQUATTING ON YOUR EXPRESSIONS.. BUT I GUESS YOU NEED A PERMANENT CHANGE-OVER. ADMINISTERED BY BLADE!
WHAT IN THE HELL IS SHE BABBLING ABOUT? SHE WOULDN'T CUT ME? YES, SHE'S CRAZY ENOUGH TO DO ANYTHING. I'VE GOT TO GET OUT OF HERE, GOT TO GET BACK TO MY OFFICE AND MAKE SOME PHONE CALLS. I'LL PUT A CONTRACT OUT ON BOTH OF THEM.. HA! THAT'S WHAT I'LL DO.

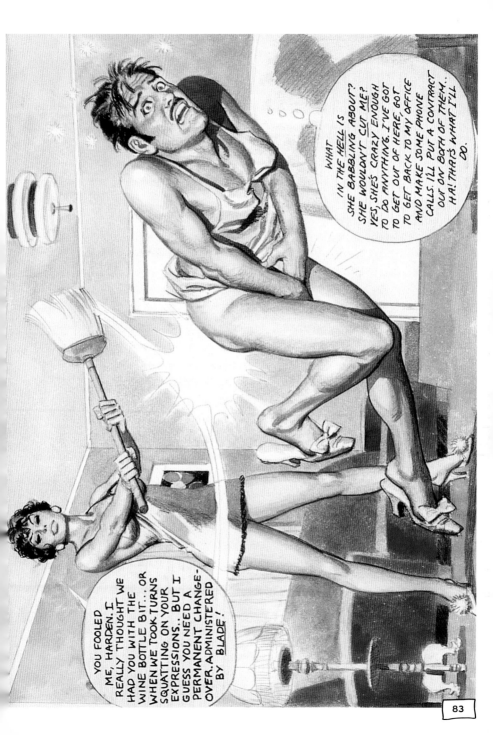

BE STILL AND LISTEN TO ME. YOU REMEMBER THE DOUGH YOU WERE HANDLING FOR CHICAGO CHARLIE? WELL YOU SIGNED IT OVER TO US.
C.. CH.. CHARLIE'LL KILL ME... IT IT'S A HUNDRED GRAND!
TOO BAD! ... AND NOW HE'S GOING TO GET AN ANONY-MOUS CALL TELLING HIM YOU... JUST GAMBLED IT AWAY.
YOU'RE A DEAD MAN! NOBODY WILL TOUCH YOU IF YOU'RE ON CHARLIE'S CHILL LIST!
MMF... FUMFPH PUFMFF PUFFER.
YOU WILL HAVE TO DO A VANISH-ING ACT, HARDEN. ... MAYBE JOIN THE OTHER BUMS ON THE STREET.
UNGF FUNK FOOR.. TOO...

I'M AN OLD FARM-GIRL, HARDEN. I STILL REMEMBER HOW THEY USED TO SPAY THE BOARS TO MAKE THEM FAT AND WELLBEHAVED. JUST A SNIP HERE, A SNIP THERE.. AND OUT THEY POP! READY?

NNN... OOO.... NNN..O D..N'T!
WHAT'S THAT YOU'RE SAYING? NOW? NOW? DO IT? I GUESS YOU'VE FINALLY DECIDED TO REFORM YOUR GIRL CHASING WAYS. AFTER THIS I GUARANTEE YOU WON'T EVEN DREAM ABOUT GIRLS.

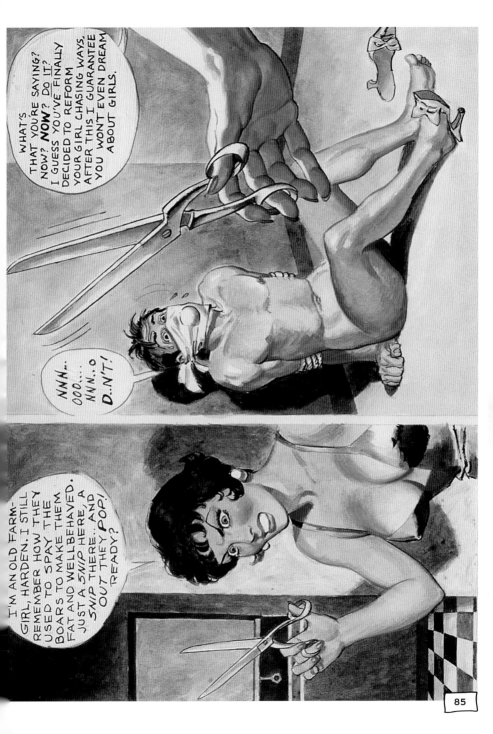

SAY GOODBYE TO THE FAMILY JEWELS. I THINK I'LL PICKLE THEM AND KEEP THEM AROUND TO REMIND ME HOW MUCH I ENJOYED **THIS!**
CLARA! WE GOT OUR MONEY BACK ALONG WITH EVERYTHING ELSE HE HAD HARDEN, IS DEAD BROKE!

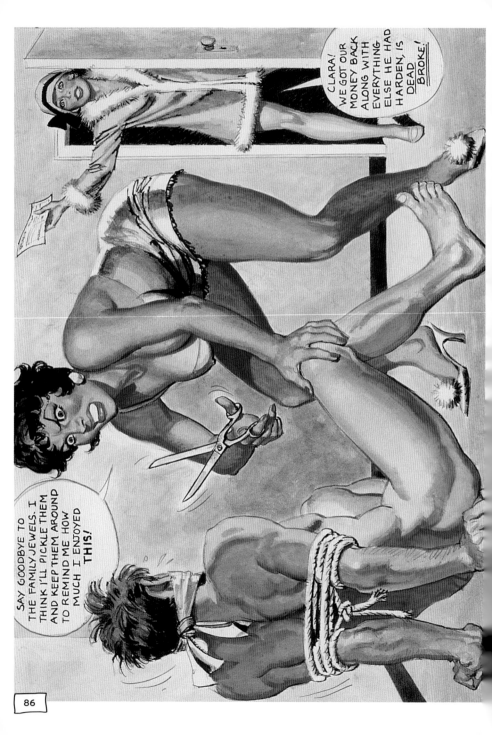

SCRAWNY BEAT-UP FAG-ASS OUT OF HERE, HARDEN, BEFORE I CHANGE MY MIND AND SNIP 'EM OFF ANYWAY!
M-MY SHORTS..I CAN'T GO AROUND NAKED UNDER THIS!
GOT TO GET TO MY APARTMENT. BUT CHICAGO CHARLIE'S BOYS WILL BE WATCHING FOR ME. MAYBE THE OFFICE... DAMN BITCHES!

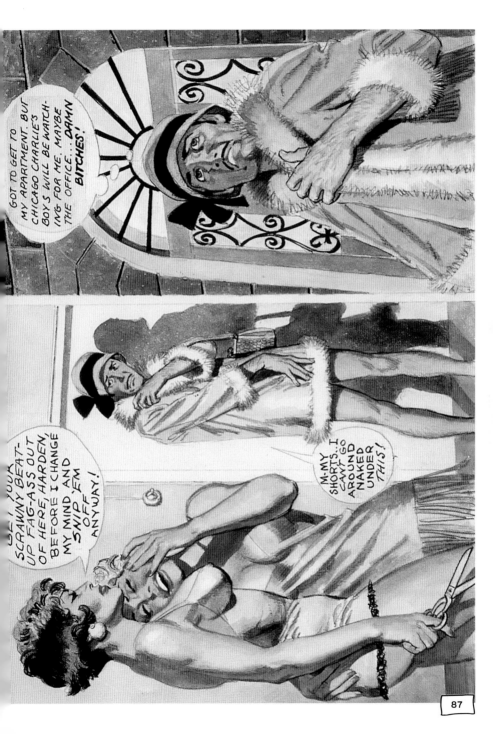

BAR
CAN'T WANDER THE STREET AIMLESS-LY. OOPS... COPS!
LASSIE, I DON'T LIKE YOUR SORT PRANCING ABOUT ON ME BEAT...NOW GIT ON...
BRSSK... BRMM... DANCING? OH... MY!

(.....)?
YOU DINNA FOOL ME LADDIE...YE JUS' BOUGHT YERSELF A TICKET TO DA CONCRETE BALLROOM.
J'JAIL? THEY'LL ASK ME WHO I AM... I DON'T EVEN HAVE AN I.D.!
IN YER GO! YER CELLMATE IS SIR QUIGLEY RAMSGATE III. BE EASY ON HER MATE... HEH! HEH!
DORIS
COP
XXX

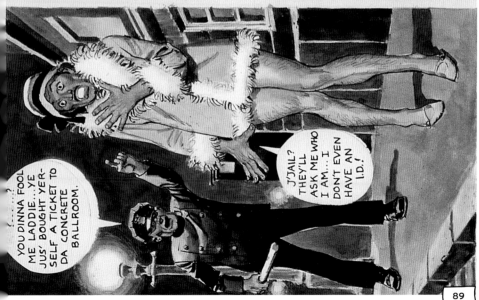

YOU, MY LITTLE THISTLEDOWN, ARE A VISION OF FEMININE PULCH-RI-TUDE. OFTEN I'VE TOLD THE TURN-KEYS THAT AN EN-LIGHTED REGIME *HIC*...
WOULD QUARTER A NOBLE... SOUL LIKE MYSELF WITH...
OH! SHUT UP, YOU HUMAN BAR RAG. I'M A RENOWNED LAWYER... NOT A... AHH.
I'VE HIT THE BOTTOM. WHAT *ELSE* COULD GO AGAINST ME? ...WHERE DO I TURN? WHO DO I LOOK TO.. FOR COMPANIONSHIP.. *LOVE*...

BETTER LEFT UNSEEN... SO LET US MOVE AHEAD SEVERAL DAYS...
BONNIE!! HEY, IT'S ME! DOUG HARDEN! I'VE GOT TO TALK TO YOU. OUR SCORE IS SETTLED... BONNIE?
YOU'VE GOT TO TELL CHICAGO CHARLIE THAT, THAT I.. DIDN'T TAKE HIS MONEY!
I DON'T KNOW YOU. TAKE YOUR FILTHY HAND...
YOU DO REMIND ME OF SOMEONE... A BASTARD WHO TOOK MY MONEY AND ALMOST ME! BUT HE'S BEEN FIXED REAL GOOD. HE DOESN'T KNOW IT YET BUT HE'S BEEN DISBARRED TOO... NOW YOU CHEEEP RUMMY... TAKE A POWDER!

YOU DIRTY PERVERT. LET GO OF ME. STOP SLOBBERING... ...ALL OVER MY NEW COAT... UGH!! YOU SMELL AWFUL!
BONNIE, THEY PUT ME IN A CELL WITH AN AWFUL MONSTER. AN'I WAS IN YOUR CLOTHES... ANDI DIDN'T HAVE ANY UNDERWEAR ON...
HE'S BEEN MAKING SUGGESTIONS ...ER OFFICER, WHAT IS CORN HOLING?
YE DONNA GIV' UP DO YER LAD... DON' WORRY MILADY I'LL HAUL 'IM AWAY ORIGHT!
KNOCK

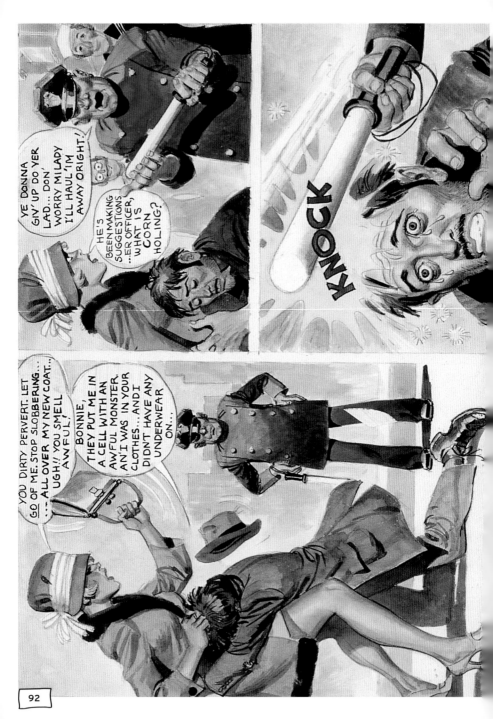

SASPARILLA! THE QUALITY OF GUESTS IN THIS ESTABLISHMENT HAS FALLEN DECIDEDLY. NO WONDER THEY NO LONGER LODGE YOUNG LADIES HERE. I REMEMBER THAT ONE POOR LASS... AND HER AWFUL LAWYER'S STORIES, OH WELL... BE A CHANGE BEDDING DOWN WITH ME OWN KIND.
THE END

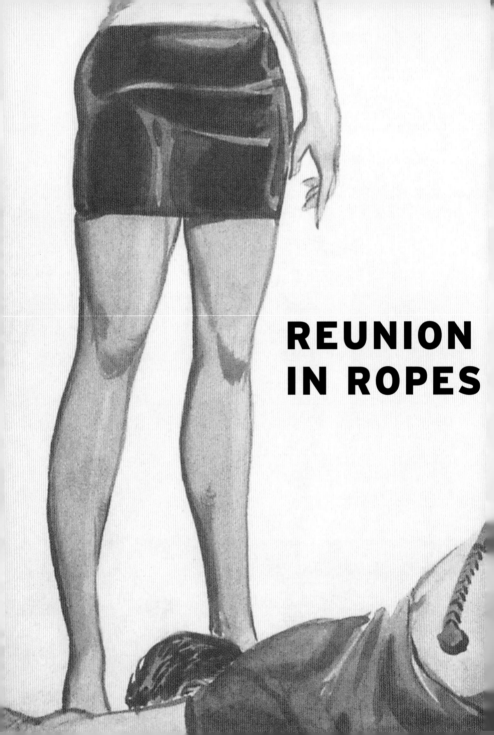

**REUNION
IN ROPES**

CAROL, I WISH YOU'D UNDERSTAND HOW MUCH THIS TRIP MEANS TO ME. I HAVEN'T SEEN DAVID SINCE HIS MARRIAGE.. AND...
..AND YOU'RE HIS BEST FRIEND! I KNOW.. YOU'VE TOLD ME A DOZEN TIMES! I.. CHRIS!! MY BRUSH!!
HOW MANY TIMES HAVE I TOLD YOU NOT TO USE THIS ON YOUR DEAD HEAD? JUST LOOK AT THIS MESS! YOU-ARE-DISGUSTING!
YOU'RE ANGRY EVER SINCE I TOLD DAVID WE'D STAY FOR THE WEEK!.. WHY?
I DON'T CARE TO GO INTO IT, CHRIS.. AT LEAST NOT NOW... IT'S WHAT YOU WANT THAT COUNTS ISN'T IT?
YOU'LL LIKE DAVID! HONEST, CAROL, HE'S A GREAT GUY! HE... IS...

HOW MUCH FURTHER IS IT TO THIS GOD FORSAKEN PLACE? I'M DRIVING HALF THE NIGHT!
WE'RE ALMOST THERE... I'M SURE! IT IS A LONG TIME..
CAROL, WOULD YOU AT LEAST PRETEND.. YOU'RE HAPPY TO BE HERE?
I'LL THINK ABOUT IT!
WE'D ABOUT GIVEN UP ON YOUR GETTING HERE! AS A RULE I DON'T WAIT UP FOR LATE GUESTS... BUT YOU MUST BE BUSHED... COME SAY GOOD-NIGHT TO DAVID.
I'M TERRIBLY SORRY, BLANCHE, BUT I DON'T DRIVE.. AND CAROL'S UNFAMILIAR WITH THE ROADS!
THANKS!

2

DAVID.. DAVID! SAY GOOD-NIGHT TO YOUR FRIENDS!
YES... YES, DON'T GET UP!.. HELLO AND GOOD-BYE!
HI, DAVID! WE MADE IT!.. GOOD TO SEE YOU AGAIN.. ..YOU LOOK.. FINE...
HELLO, CHRIS.. CAROL... ER.. BLANCHE WILL SHOW YOU YOUR ROOM.. WE'LL ..CHAT.. IN THE MORNING!

I'M SO HAPPY YOU COULD COME, CAROL, REALLY! I WAS ALL WEEK PREPARING... CLEANING YOUR ROOM. I DO HOPE YOUR STAY WILL AT LEAST BE INTERRESTING!
OOHH!? YOU SHOULDN'T HAVE BOTHERED, REALLY!
BREAKFAST WILL BE AT 9! WE CAN GET BETTER ACQUAINTED THEN!
GREAT... ALL THIS WAY AND THE LAZY... HE DIDN'T EVEN GET OFF HIS--
SHH! CAROL, NOT SO LOUD!
I KNOW ITS WIERD BUT... WAIT UNTIL TO-MORROW. THINGS WILL BE FINE. YOU'LL SEE
WOULDN'T EVEN GET OFF HIS ASS!

DO YOU HEAR THAT...THAT MOANING!?
WHAT ELSE DO YOU THINK I'VE BEEN LISTENING TO FOR THE LAST HOUR? IT MUST BE THE DOG!
NO! BLANCHE WOULDN'T HAVE A PET IN THE HOUSE!
NOO! WHAT WAS THAT THING THAT SAT GREETING US!?
MOAN
I'LL BE DAMNED IF I'LL PUT UP WITH IT ANY LONGER... COME, CHRIS!
NO... CAROL.. WAIT!

MR. DUNNING... TAKE YOUR HANDS OFF ME..
CAROL, IF YOU DON'T BEHAVE.. I'LL...
OH!.. WHAT, CHRIS... WHAT WILL YOU DO TO ME?.. SPANK ME? OF COURSE... BE BRUTAL, DARLING, IT IS YOUR WAY OF SETTLING THINGS!
DON'T... PUSH.. CAROL!
OOH!
C-CHRIS?
D..D..DAVID!

WAIT CAROL, I KNOW DAVE... THERE'S SOMETHING WRONG! HE WOULDN'T KNEEL THERE ON HIS HAUNCHES, BARE-ASSED LIKE A DOG UNLESS....
UNLESS TO FURTHER ANTAGONIZE ME! WELL, IF YOU DON'T WANT TO SEE YOUR..BUDDY... KICKED IN HIS... OH! LET'S GET THE HELL OUT OF THIS HOUSE!
AS THEY TURN TO LEAVE, DAVID SHUDDERS.. ..TRIES TO RAISE HIMSELF. THE ROBE SLIPS FROM HIS SHOULDERS.

GOOD CHRIST, DAVE...WHO... DID THIS....? CAROL, CALL BLANCHE!
NM..MMN NOoo.
HE CAN HARDLY TALK! LIFT HIM UP!

STEADY.. HOLD HIM STEADY!
DON'T STAND THERE WORRYING ABOUT HOLDING HIM STILL! UNTIE HIM!
DID I... HEAR RIGHT? DID HE SAY DON'T FREE HIM!?
THAT'S WHAT THE MAN SAID!
NOO... NO. D.. DON'T FREE. MEEE!
OH!... YOU POOR GUY! CAROL, WILL YOU LOOK AT THIS!

BLANCHE... YOU DID THIS...
OF COURSE! HE WAS.. NAUGHTY.. I HAVE TO PUNISH HIM.. SIMPLE AS THAT! NOW IF YOU'LL BOTH GO BACK TO BED, I'LL SEE TO IT HE DOESN'T DISTURB US ANY FURTHER!
THAT DID IT! WE'RE NOT SPENDING THE NIGHT IN AN ASYLUM!
I CAN'T LEAVE NOW, CAROL! I'LL HAVE TO HELP DAVID EVEN IF HE DOESN'T WANT IT!
DON'T TELL ME YOU'RE ACTUALLY GOING TO...
..TO SPANK HIM... ACTUALLY, YES!

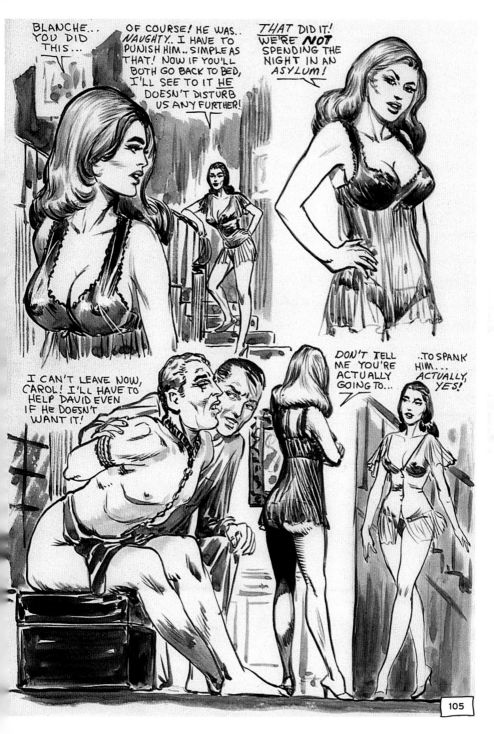

..AND RIGHT NOW IS AS GOOD A TIME AS ANY. YOU CAN UNTIE HIM IF YOU'D LIKE... IF YOU CAN..THAT IS...
UNTIE HIM YOURSELF! AS FAR AS I'M CONCERNED, YOU CAN BEAT HIM TILL HE BLEADS!
I INTEND TO DO JUST THAT! WOULD YOU MIND?.. ...STEPPING ASIDE....
I'LL DO BETTER THAN THAT.. I... CHRIS! DON'T YOU DARE UNTIE HIM!
CAROL, YOU DON'T WANT ME TO LEAVE HIM HERE... ..LIKE THIS?

CHRISTOPHER... DID HE... ONCE ASK YOUR HELP?
BUT... BUT... NOO! I.. I GUESS YOU ARE... RIGHT!
AH, DAVID.. NOW THAT YOUR... FRIEND..? IS LEAVING.. WE CAN GET ON WITH IT. POSITION YOURSELF... BEFORE ME... BEND OVER... THAT'S IT... A LITTLE MORE... YES!
OH.. NO... I CAN'T STAND THIS.. I BETTER GO.. DOWN!..
CRACK
YIEE
YOU'D BETTER MIND YOUR OWN!
GET DRESSED!

OH.. CAROL! BEFORE YOU LEAVE, I'D LIKE A FEW WORDS WITH YOU...
CONCERNING? CHRIS... I'M WAITING!
LOOK, I'M SORRY ABOUT THIS, HONEST! THIS SHOW WAS NOT MY IDEA! DAVID PLANNED THE WHOLE SCENE.. YOU SEE HE LIKES IT!.. ..THE DOMINATION BIT... AND.. HE SAYS CHRIS DOES TOO!
WHAT? ARE YOU... SAYING.. THAT ...MY... NOOO.... NO! THEY ARE FRIENDS! BUT...
BLANCHE... IF CHRIS... DIGS THIS.. AND IS... HIDING IT FROM ME... I WANT TO KNOW!
LEAVE IT TO ME! I KNOW ONE WHEN SEE ONE...
IT IS LATE CHRIS AND I DO HAVE SO MUCH TO DO!
C..CAROL, I'D BETTER SEE DAVID, FIRST!
NO! CHRIS! YOUR.. FRIEND... PLANNED THIS.. ..THIS THING.. TO GET US TO PARTICIPATE! HE'S.. HE'S A...A.. MASOCHIST!

DAVID.. YOU HEARD. IS IT TRUE? YOU... WANTED THIS..
I.. CHRIS... I...
IT'S TRUE IT IS! BLANCHE IS RIGHT. ADMIT IT! MAKE HIM ADMIT IT!
YES, DOO!
ALL RIGHT, DAVID, YOU WANTED US TO PLAY IN YOUR LITTLE GAME. WE'LL PLAY! YOU GOT US ALL THE WAY OUT HERE SO YOU COULD PRACTISE YOUR RELIGION.. I'M NOT GOING TO LET YOU DOWN...NO, NO! I'M GOING TO BEAT YOU WITHIN AN INCH OF YOUR LIFE. CHRIS, BEND HIM OVER YOUR KNEE!
CAROL, THIS IS NONE OF OUR BUSINESS. I'M NOT GOING TO TAKE A HAND IN THIS!
BEND OVER! ...FOR CAROL, DAVID!

DAVEY DOESN'T WANT ANYONE ORDERING HIM ABOUT BUT ME! ISN'T THAT RIGHT? TELL THEM, DAVID, DEAR!
I DON'T WANT ANYONE TELLIN... HEY!!
CAROL! YOU WERE IN A HURRY TO LEAVE... SO.. LET'S GO!
I'M SURE DAVID WANTS YOU TO STAY...
CHOKE! YES YES, DAMN IT STAY!!
ONLY IF YOU SAY PLEASE, DAVEY! YOU DO KNOW HOW TO BEG, DON'T YOU? BEG... DAVID! BEG ME TO STAY! BEG ME TO DOMINATE YOU!
TELL'EM TO GO TO HELL DAVID!

CAROL, FOR GOD'S SAKE DON'T DO THIS!
OH FOR... IF YOU'RE SO ANXIOUS TO HELP HIM, WHY THE HELL DON'T YOU OFFER TO TAKE HIS PLACE... OR IS THAT WHERE.. FRIENDSHIP... ENDS!?
YOU HAVEN'T SAID PLEASE, DAVID... YOU WILL SAY IT WON'T YOU?
NKT! PLKT!

THIS IS YOUR LAST CHANCE TO SAVE YOUR BEST FRIEND! MAKE UP YOUR MIND, CHRIS... WOULD YOU CARE TO DRAPE YOURSELF ACROSS BLANCHE'S LAP AND TAKE DAVID'S PUNISHMENT? HE'D DO IT FOR YOU!! WOULDN'T YOU, DAVID!
YES! YES!
WELL... HE.. LIKES IT!

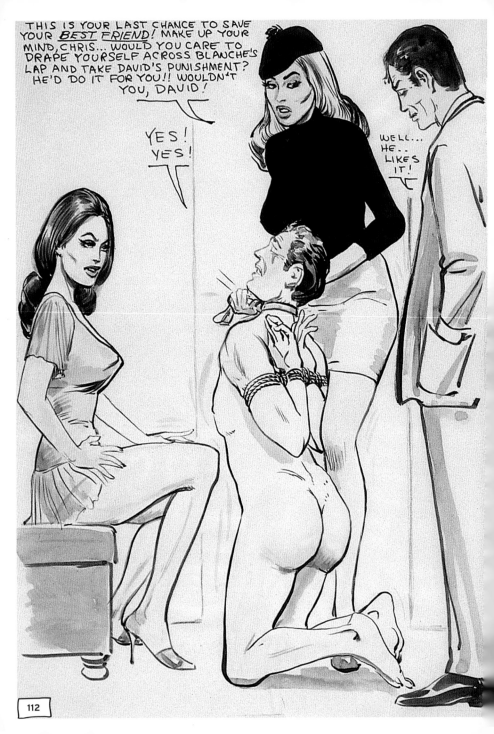

THERE! DO YOU LIKE IT BETTER WHEN I HIT YOU? DON'T I HIT *HARDER* THAN BLANCHE?
OOH!.. *AGAIN!* *MAKE HIM JUMP!* OOH!
CHRIS! *PLEASE!*
I'M SORRY DAVID..BUT YOU PLANNED IT THIS WAY. YOU *LIKE* IT!

CHRIS! CHRIS! OW! IT.. ITS HER! BLANCHE! SHE'S THE ONE... LOOOK... LOOK AT... HER... FACE!
STOP OOOH! CAROL OOEEEE... ENOUGH!
IT'S O.K. DAVE.. I I UNDERSTAND.. ITS NOTHING TO BE ASHAMED OF!

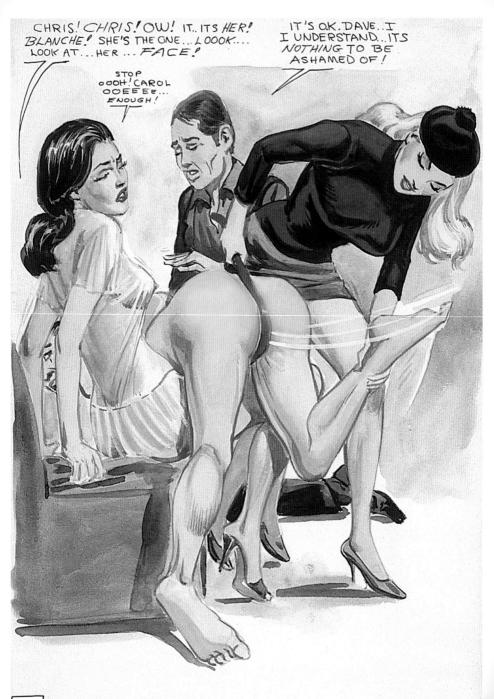

..PUFF.. STOP? WHY?
I MIGHT AS WELL OWN UP, CAROL! DAVID'S RIGHT!.. ITS ME! I'M THE ONE!!..YEP! MY THING!
THERE, SEE, I TOLD YOU! I KNEW I WAS RIGHT... ABOUT DAVE! YOU, YOU'RE SO DAMN SMART! WHAT ARE YOU GOING TO DO NOW?
UNTIE ME! UNTIE ME!
YAHOO! GOOD GIRL! I KNEW YOU WERE WITH ME!
I... HEY! CAROL QUIT...
ALL THE WAY BLANCHE! RIGHT FROM THE START! ALL THE WAY!

LATER.-
I CAN NOW UNDERSTAND YOUR...ER... KICKS, BLANCHE? I WAS...STIMULATED FOR AWHILE THERE. A SENSATION I.. NEVER FELT BEFORE!
MM HMNN! NOTHING LIKE IT! TAKING A PROUD MAN DOWN, KEEPING HIM HELP-LESS, PLEADING... AND HURTING! MM. GOOSE BUMPS!
IT..IS.. ESPECIALLY GOOD WITH A MAN WHO DOESN'T WANT TO SUBMIT!
CHRIS... HE'D NEVER SUBMIT. HOW WOULD YOU GO ABOUT BRINGING HIM DOWN? HE'S QUITE STRONG AND HE IS AWARE OF YOUR... THING?
HMM! HE WOULD BE A CHALLENGE! I DO HAVE YOUR PER-MISSION TO.. TRY... I GATHER! YES...IN THE... MORNING?

NEXT MORNING
BLANCHE, I WANT YOU TO KNOW I DON'T APPROVE OF..OF LAST NIGHT! I UNDERSTAND THESE THINGS...ABOUT PEOPLE ENJOYING B&D! BUT..ONLY WHEN BOTH PARTYS AGREE! DAVID IS AGAINST IT! I DON'T LIKE TO BUTT INTO MARRIED PEOPLES..BUT..
THEN DON'T DARLING... STAY OUT OF IT!
LOOK, MR. DUNNING! I'VE JUST ABOUT HAD ENOUGH INTERFERANCE FROM YOU. IF YOU DON'T LIKE WHAT TRANSPIERS IN MY HOME, WHY DON'T YOU SIMPLY GET THE HELL OUT!
OH, YOU'D LIKE THAT! BUT I'VE GOT NEWS FOR YOU... I'M STAYING! DAVID'S NOT GOING TO PLAY YOUR LITTLE GAMES ANY LONGER.. NOT IF I HAVE ANYTHING TO SAY ABOUT IT. I DON'T GIVE ONE GOD DAMN IF I AM A GUEST OR NOT!
I...SEE... HERE'S DAVINA, OUR NEW MAID WITH..BREAKFAST!
22

..AND FURTHERMORE BLANCHE.. I'D ADVISE YOU TO SEE A GOOD PSYCHO AS SOON AS POSSIBLE!
CHRIS!!? APOLOGIZE TO BLANCHE. YOU HAVE NO RIGHT TO SAY THAT!
THANK YOU, DAVINA... THAT WILL BE ALL! YOU MAY ATTEND TO THE MATTER UPSTAIRS. - NOW!
BECAUSE I'M A WOMAN YOU, YOU THINK YOU CAN INTERFERE AND INSULT ME! THAT I WON'T FIGHT YOU.. THAT ONLY A MAN WOULD STRIKE YOU. I DON'T WONDER HOW YOU'D REACT IF I WERE A MAN!
IF YOU WERE A MAN... I'D THRASH YOU WITHIN AN INCH OF YOUR LIFE!
DON'T LET SEX STOP YOU DEAR! LET ME SEE YOU IN ACTON! THRASH HER! SHE HAS CHALLENGED YOU!
HE DOESN'T HAVE THE GUTS, BLANCHE. I DON'T THINK HE'S MAN ENOUGH TO ATTACK ANYONE! I WONDER IF HE HAS THE COURAGE TO DE-FEND HIMSELF?
CAROL, IF I'M RROVOKED FURTHER BY EITHER OF YOU, I WON'T BE RESPONSIBLE FOR MY ACTIONS!

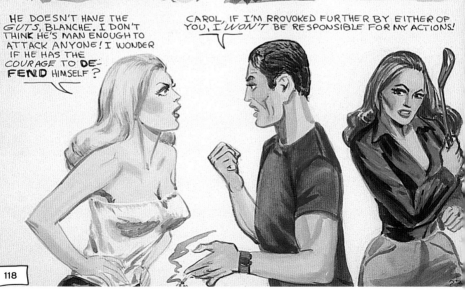

IS THIS PROVOCATION?
YIEEEE!
YOU BITCH!
OH!

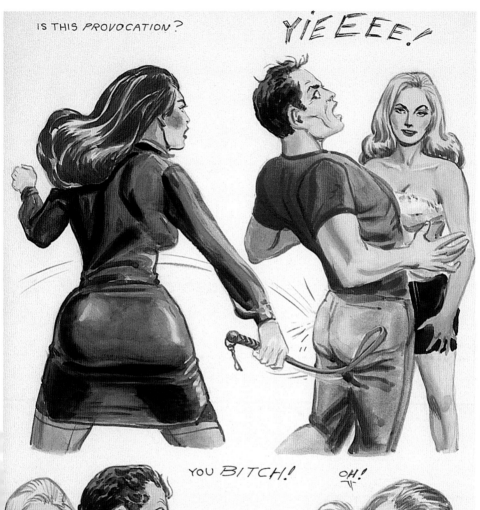

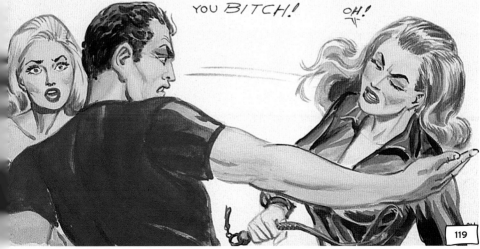

HEY, YOU'RE GOOD! REALLY GOOD! ONE SWING AND YOU DRAW BLOOD!
CHRIS, YOU'RE THE SADIST! FIRST YOU INSULT THEN...
DAMN IT, CAROL.. YOU KNOW HOW I FEEL ABOUT GETTING HIT.. IN THE BACK.. I DON'T LIKE IT.. MY MOTHER....
THE NON-VIOLENT HUBBY TURNS OUT TO BE OF ALL THINGS, A WOMAN HATER! WORSE YET, HE PROBABLY HIT HIS MOMMY!
CHRIS! WHEN YOUR MOTHER SPANKED YOU... ...YOU HIT.. HER... BACK?
YOU BASTARD!
25

STOP THIS CAROL...I DON'T WANT TO HEAR ANY-MORE!
WHAT ARE YOU GOING TO DO? BEAT ME UP? I'M NOT AN OLD HELPLESS WOMAN LIKE YOUR MOTHER! I CAN HIT BACK!
WOULD GET SOME ROPE FROM THE STUDY WHILE I UNDRESS MR.HARDHEAD... HURRY BEFORE HE COMES TOO! I DIDN'T HIT HIM HARD ENOUGH!
26

GOOD, JUNIOR'S COME BACK TO US IN TIME TO HEAR THE *RULES* OF OUR LITTLE GAME!
OH.. MY HEAD! CAROL! WHERE'S OH.. CAROL? OW! YOU... *BITCHES!*
RIGHT *HERE*, CHRIS! WE'RE GOING TO HELP YOU DARLING.... ...YOU'RE GOING TO RELIVE YOUR CHILDHOOD TO GET TO THE BOTTOM OF YOUR MENTAL PROBLEMS! YOU CAN'T GO AROUND THE REST OF YOUR LIFE... *HURTING WOMEN!*

YOU WILL LEARN *NOT* TO TALK BACK WHEN *REPREMANDED!*... AND
CRACK!
...TO RESTRAIN YOUR UNCONSCIOUS DESIRE TO STRIKE *BACK* WHEN BEING PUNISHED!
CAROL! SHE'S CRAZY! STOP *THIS!!*

NOW, YOU'RE **NOT** GOING TO BE A SPOILED BRAT AND *RUIN* **MY** DAY, *JUNIOR!* I PLANNED A GREAT DEAL TO GET YOU HERE...TO CONVINCE FIRST DAVID, THEN CAROL THAT **YOU NEED** TO BE HELPED THROUGH DISCIPLINE! ...TO BE TIED UP LIKE THIS SO YOU'LL BE ABLE TO FEEL LIKE A LITTLE BOY AGAIN!
YOU'RE GOING *TOO* **ROUGH!**..FAR... ..BLANCHE! I'LL GET FREE AND THEN....
WHEN **WE** DECIDE TO RELEASE YOU, YOU WILL HAVE BEEN PROPERLY TRAINED AND WELL BEHAVED AS IS YOUR PRECIOUS SWEET *DAVID!*

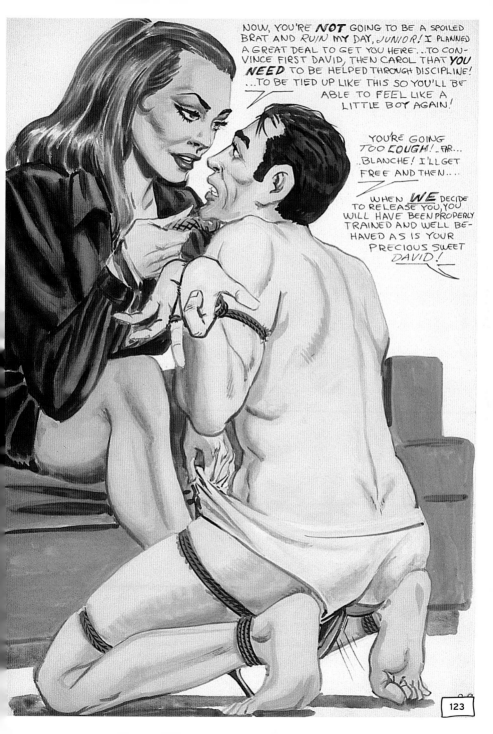

MY, WHAT SATINY SKIN HE HAS! I CAN SEE WHY HE DISLIKES BEING VIOLATED THERE! IT'S SO TENDER... SO SOFT...SO CARED FOR...THAT WILL HAVE TO BE CHANGED! WON'T IT CAROL?
A MAN'S DERRIER SHOULD NO BE SO.. IT SHOULD AND WILL BE TREATED... TOUGHENED! MAY I BORROW YOUR DOG-STRAP?
TAKE YOUR HANDS OFF ME! CAROL... BLANCHE!... DON'T DO IT! DON'T GET ME MAD! D-DAVID... DAVID!

WAIT UNTIL I GET A FIRM GRIP....OKAY! READY! MAKE THE FIRST ONE A GOOD ONE. DON'T MISS!
MISS?... THAT TARGET?
WAIT!
HOLD IT! OOHWEE! LOOK AT THE MARK ONE SHOT LEFT! HE'S NOT GOING TO BE ABLE TO TAKE MUCH. I DON'T WANT TO MISS MY CHANCE. LET'S ALTERNATE!
OH NO! UH UNH! I'LL NOT STOP NOW. I'M BEGINNING TO WARM UP TO IT!
OH!
31

CAROL!! WHY HAVE YOU STOPPED? ARE YOU ALL RIGHT?
ALL RIGHT?...OOH...OH! I NEVER FELT THIS GOOD! OH... SEN... SATIONAL ...THE THROBBING! OH.. GOD...OOH OH!

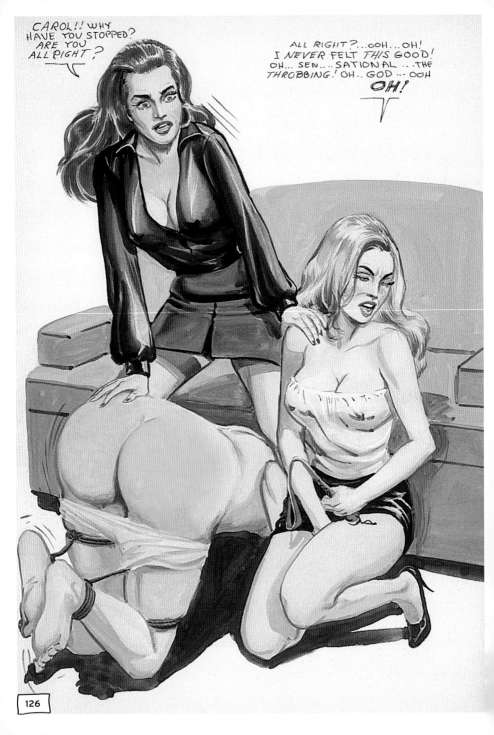

OH... BLANCHE... UNTIE HIM.... I'VE GOT TO.... HAVE HIM...
NOW BE FAIR CAROL! IF WE'RE TO REMAIN FRIENDS, YOU'VE GOT TO SHARE... YOU WHIPPED HIM. LET ME HAVE HIM!
YOU...(OH! MY BACK..) BLANCHE! YOU.. YOU'RE NOT! CAROL YOU CAN'T PERMIT IT! I WON'T DO IT! I..I WON'T GET EXCITED!
OH, YES YOU WILL! YOU WILL IF YOU KNOW WHAT'S GOOD FOR YOU! I WON'T BE MADE A FOOL OF... UNDERSTAND!?
CHRIS!! DON'T YOU DARE GET EXCITED! YOU SWORE YOU NEVER CHEAT! IF YOU REALLY LOVE ME.. PROVE IT NOW!
33

WE'LL SEE HOW GOOD HE IS! DO YOU OBEY CAROL OR.. I! CHOOSE.. WISELY!?
HA HA... IF I... SAID PLEASE... DAMN IT!.. WOULD YOU STOP THIS?
HA HA NO! OH! HA HA HA
WHAT. THE HELL ARE YOU LAUGHING AT.... OH! NO WONDER! TICKLING IS NOT FAIR! CAROL!
ALL'S FAIR, DEAR... IN LOVE.. ..AND.. THIS IS WAR!

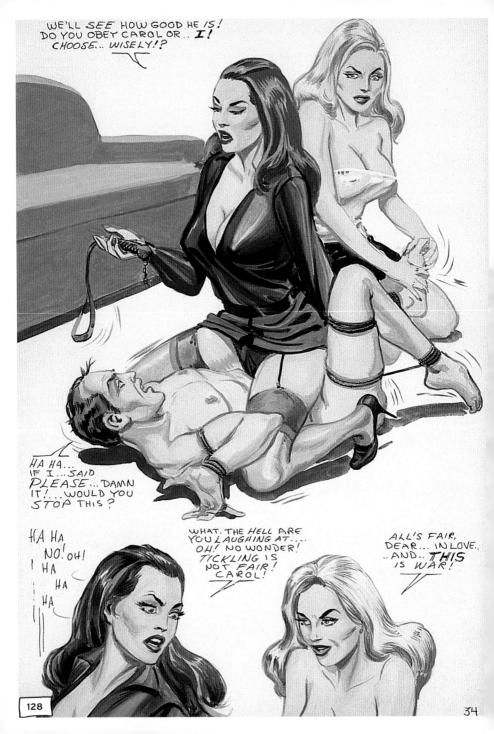

YIEE!.. CHRIS! IF YOU DARE!? CHRIS!! YOU BASTARD... I MEAN IT! DON'T YOU DARE!
TOO.. LATE... I'VE WON! I KNEW... IT! I KNOW MY... MEN... DARLING... I.... KNOW... OH... OH..
DAVID... A QUIET WITNESS TO CHRIS'S RAPE....
YOU!! THIS IS YOUR FAULT! IF YOU WERE ANY KIND OF MAN.. THIS WOULDN'T HAVE.... HAPPEN. (SOB) PENNED.... I HATE THE SIGHT OF... YOU! I OUGHT TO... OH! CHRIST! I'VE NEVER BEEN SO.. SO HURT.... I... I COULD KILL YOU....
The End

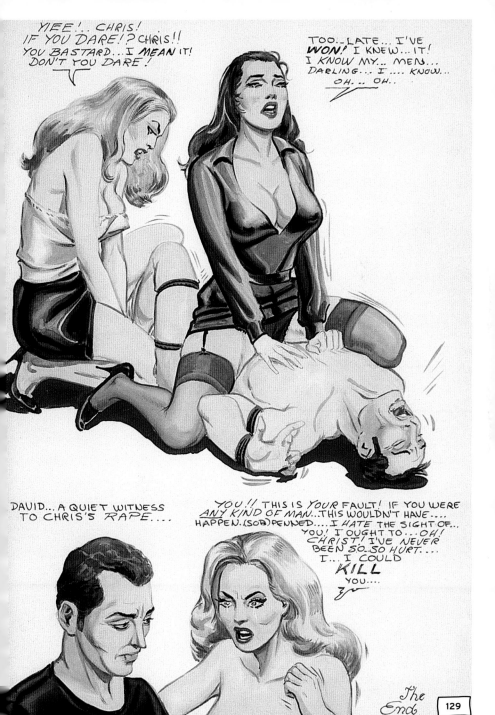

THE
DOMINANT
WIVES

THE DOMINANT WIVES 1

Jasper Penrose is taking the train home from work, but he is not reading the paper he holds in his hands. He is re-living certain scenes from the past week involving his wife Laura. Occasionally he gingerly pats his face - left cheek, right cheek - still sore! His indignation rises, and his determination to put her in her place, once and for all! When he first started going out with Laura, she was so meek and adoring---then, right after she blushingly agreed to marry him, thats when her damn hand - trouble started

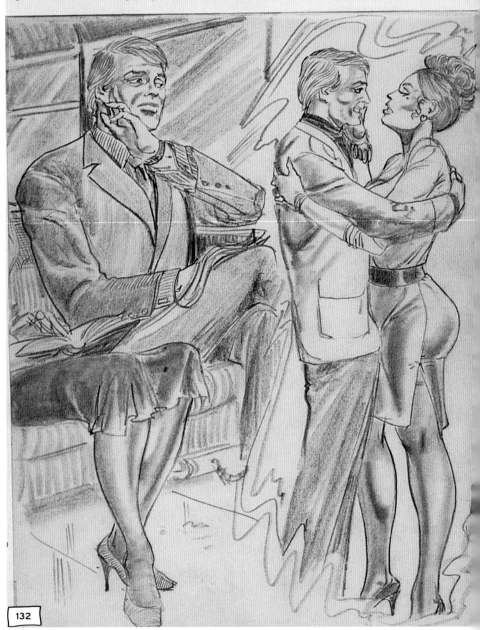

Jasper can see it now, the first time she slapped him. They were discussing where to go on their honeymoon. He favored the mountains she wanted Hawaii - then, [CRACK], she ends the argument. "WE'RE GOING TO HAWAII, AND THATS FINAL!" Holding his sting cheek Jasper is too stunned to argue. "YES DEAR" he agrees. "I THOUGHT YOU'D SEE IT MY WAY DEAR--" she replies acidly.

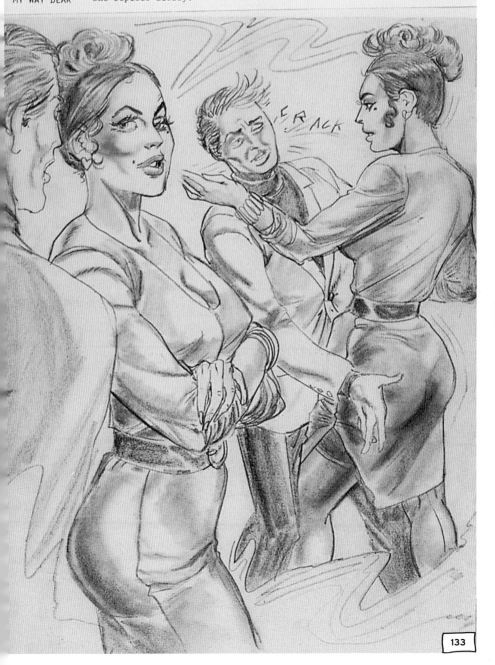

That was only the beginning. Over the passing years, it steadily got worse - the nagging, the sarcasm, the orders, and the slaps! And she doled out her sexual favors in accordance with his behavior...if he pleased her through docile obedience to her orders, she would permit him to enter her bed - then again, she might not! Lately especially, she had been getting an awful lot of migraine headaches. Riding the train home, Jasper's mind goes back to the beginning of the week - an especially disasterous week...

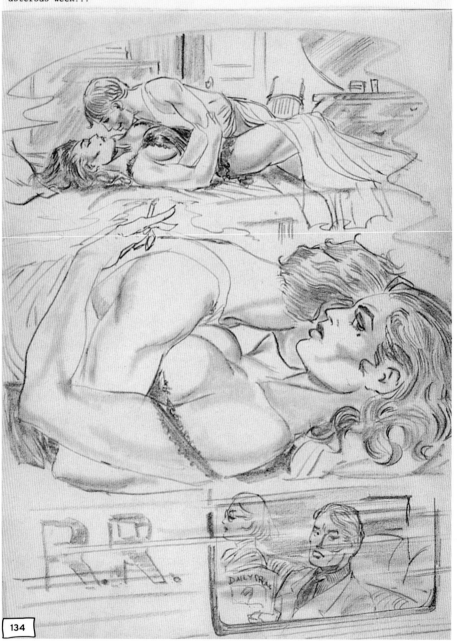

MONDAY: He forgot to put out the trash. She had told him to put out the trash the night before, so as not to miss the early Monday morning pick-up, but he had refused, saying he couldn't carry out the trash wearing his best Sunday suit, and that he'd do it first thing in the morning.

Next morning while still in their bath-robes, they heard the trash truck go by too late to put out the trash. "THAT'S ANOTHER TWO DAYS THE GARBAGE WILL STINK UP THE HOUSE, THANKS TO YOU--"[CRACK] The red blotch on his cheek had lasted all day...

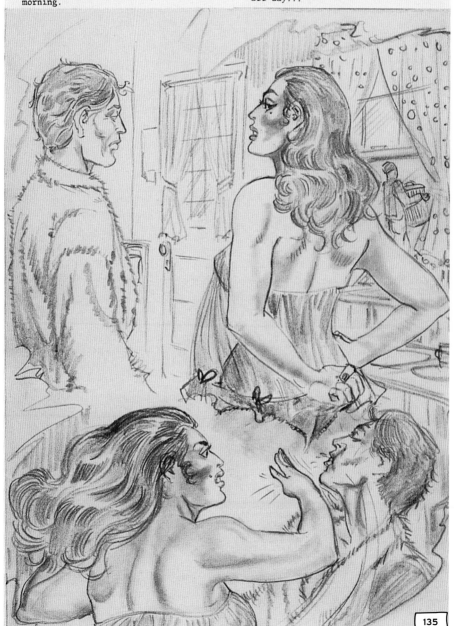

TUESDAY: Before leaving for work, she reminded him again to see Hanrahan (his boss) about his raise, and not to take "NO" for an answer. When he came home, first thing she said was "WELL, DID YOU TALK TO MR. HANRAHAN, LIKE I TOLD YOU?" "WELL, he explained, I STARTED TO, BUT HE WAS ON HIS WAY OUT, AND HE SAID IT WOULD HAVE TO WAIT. HE HAD THAT NEW SECRETARY ON HIS ARM, AND I THINK THEY WERE GOING TO THAT NEW APARTMENT HE FIXED UP FOR HER--"

"NEVER MIND THAT BULLSHIT!" she interrupted angerly. "YOU HAVEN'T HAD A RAISE IN TWO YEARS AND I NEED A NEW FUR COAT! ARE YOU OR AREN'T YOU GOING TO DEMAND THAT RAISE TOMORROW?" She stepped closer and placed her hand on her hip (always a danger sign) "WELL, I WOULD, DEAR,.. HONEST, BUT I THINK HE'S GOING TO SPEND A WEEK WITH HER IN THAT APARTMENT..." Laura's lips curled in disgust. "THAT'S THE STORY OF YOUR LIFE, JASPER." [CRACK]!..The bright red outline of her hand springs up on his cheek "AND DON'T BOTHER COMING TO BED TONIGHT. YOU'VE GIVEN ME A HEADACHE. YOU'LL SLEEP IN THE DEN - THE REST OF THE WEEK, TOO!"

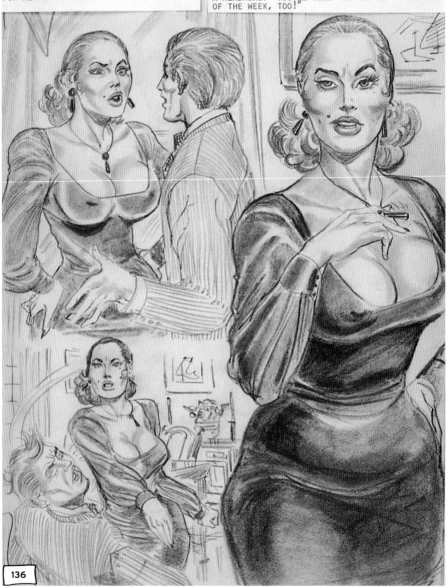

WEDNESDAY: The worst day yet. Jasper remembers every painful detail vividly. Laura had been nagging him for days to hang up that Picasso lithograph. He hated Picasso and kept putting it off. But now she was getting impatient and insisted he do it then and there. He was running out of excuses. "OH, GET OFF MY BACK, LAURA! I'M TOO TIRED. I HAD A HARD DAY AT THE OFFICE." "REALLY, DEAR? I'VE GOT JUST THE THING FOR THAT TIRED FEELING. COME CLOSER, AND I'LL GIVE YOU A SAMPLE.." Unsuspecting, he does as she says, unmindfull of her hand-on-hip posture. [CRACK] she slaps him so hard his head snaps back. "THERE - THAT WOKE YOU UP A BIT? THAT'S MY SPECIAL WAKE-UP REMEDY. WANT ANOTHER SAMPLE? [CRACK]

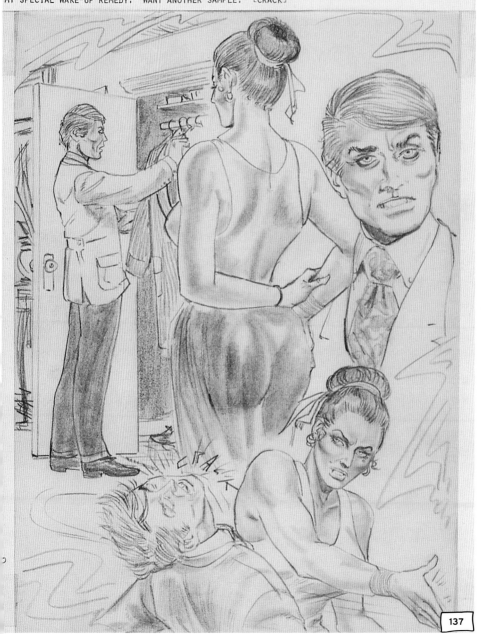

137

"YOU LOOK MUCH LIVELIER NOW, DEAR. STILL TO TIRED TO HANG UP THE PICTURE? NO, I SEE YOU'RE NOT. MY, YOU CAN REALLY MOVE WHEN YOU WANT TO, DEER." Jasper hastily begins preparations to hang up the Picasso, gathering the step-stool, hammer, picture wire, nails, etc., under her amused eyes. Leaving the room, she tells him to take his time and hang it exactly right, and to call her when its ready. She wants to get the full effect when she enters the room.

In his dazed condition Jasper picks the nail-spot and taps it in place. Then he hangs the picture - but somehow the hammer slips and bang! There's a hole right in the middle. Jasper's in a state of shock, but it's mild compared to Laura's expression when she walks into the room and sees the puncture in her prized lithograph. "M-M-MY HANDS S-SLIPPED" he explains fearfully. "WELL, MINE WON'T!" she replies grimly. "COME HERE, JASPER."

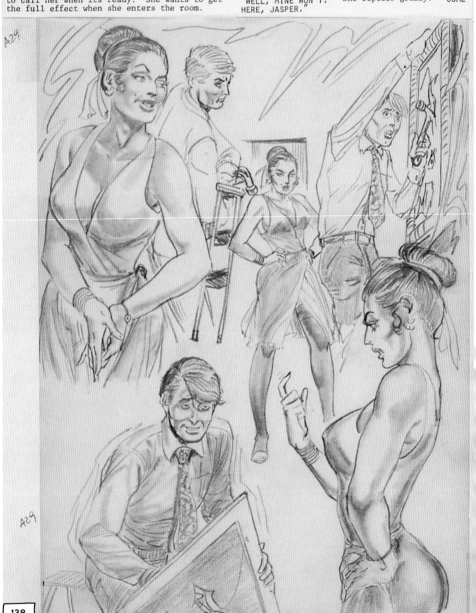

Once again he approaches his big lovely wife - but this time he is all too aware of what's in store. When he comes within striking distance, he abjectly makes a surprising request: "P-PLEASE, DEAR, NOT THE SAME CHEEK!" "WHA?" she asks. "YOU S-S-SLAPPED MY LEFT SIDE TWICE ALREADY, AND IT'S AWFULLY SORE. C-COULD YOU PLEASE USE YOUR LEFT HAND THIS TIME DEAR? "OH, ALL RIGHT. HOLD STILL!

[CRACK]!---[CRACK]!---[CRACK]!

Three times her left palm stings his right cheek. Grunting and groaning, he keeps his arms at his sides, making no attempt to ward off the blows. "NOW I'LL NEED A NEW PICASSO, AS WELL AS THAT FUR COAT, SO YOU DAMN SURE BETTER GET THAT RAISE DAMN QUICK - UNDERSTAND, FOOL?

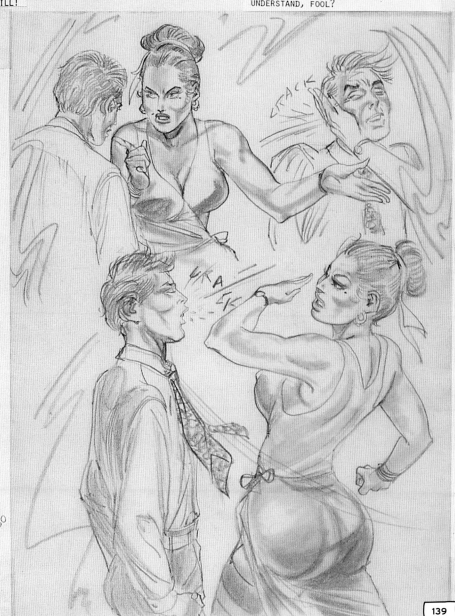

A30

[CRACK]! She back - hands his left cheek with her right this time, drawing a howl of anguish from her husband...

THURSDAY: Now it's the present, and Jasper is mentally reviewing the previous three humiliating days, especially the day before. He can't get over his shameful behavior, actually offering her his cheek to slap - begging her to slap it instead of the other-- such a degrading, timid surrender! Well, tonight, she was due for a big surprise! He'd been dwelling on it all day - his cowardice, his fear. And he has made up his mind - he isn't going to let her get away with it another day.

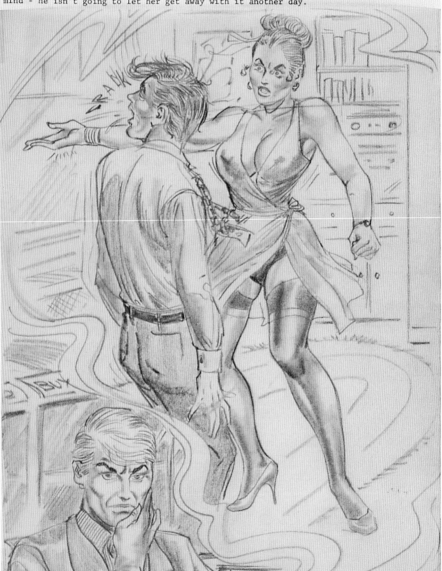

After tonight, their roles would be reversed - he would be the head of the household, his rightful role - again. Any slapping to be done, he would do it! In fact, he'll start right off by giving her one across the chops - see how she liked it. Then he ll explain how things were going to be a lot different from now on - especially that ess of sleeping in the den.

The train reaches Jasper's stop. Good! He can't wait to start laying down the law! As Jasper walks the two blocks from the train station to his house, he rehearses mentally how he should best confront Laura. In one scenario, - he walks in and belts her one - just like that. Then he lays down the law, while she listens in shocked silence ---- in another scene, he grabs her by the shoulder and shoves her down into a chair, telling her to shut up for a change and listen while he explains how things are going to be a lot different from now on --- He decides the first way is best ---

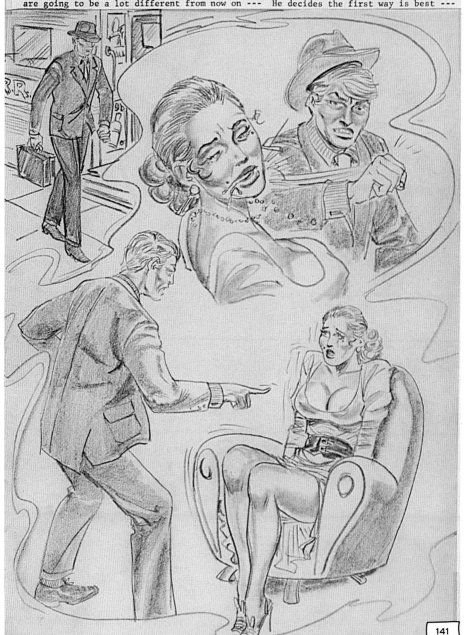

Jasper passes by the supermarket and stops in to buy six frozen TV dinners. That's another sore point he means to clear up - no more damn TV dinners - from now on she'll cook a decent meal for him everyday! Another thing - no more sleeping in the den for him - it was wrecking their love life! Jasper's fury mounts with each step he takes! He's so mad, he decides to walk up to their third floor apartment, instead of waiting for the elevator. Reaching the second floor he sees the new couple entering their apartment. They're the Johnsons - a young couple who just moved in about a week ago, the ones with the nasty habit of playing that loud rock music at odd hours day and night, making Laura's headaches even worse.... He decides to introduce himself and complain about the noise. But as he draws nearer, he forgets all about complaining. He gapes enthralled at the back view of Mrs. Johnson.

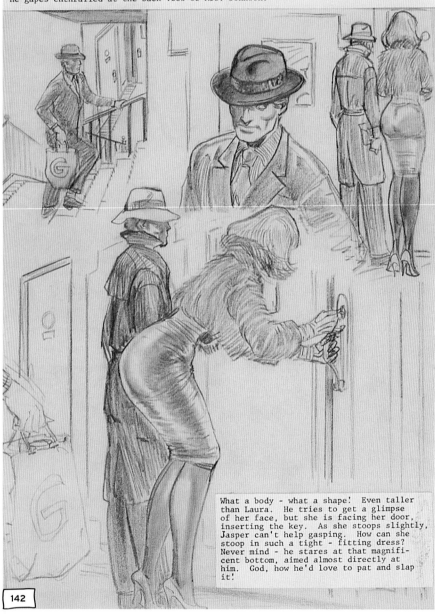

What a body - what a shape! Even taller than Laura. He tries to get a glimpse of her face, but she is facing her door, inserting the key. As she stoops slightly, Jasper can't help gasping. How can she stoop in such a tight - fitting dress? Never mind - he stares at that magnificent bottom, aimed almost directly at him. God, how he'd love to pat and slap it!

142

Now he can hear their conversation - Mrs. Johnson is berating her husband, and he is trying to soothe her wrath. But she is having none of it. "JUST WAIT TILL I GET YOU INSIDE!" she snaps as her hand reaches out and grips her husbands ear, jerking him inside and slamming the door behind them!

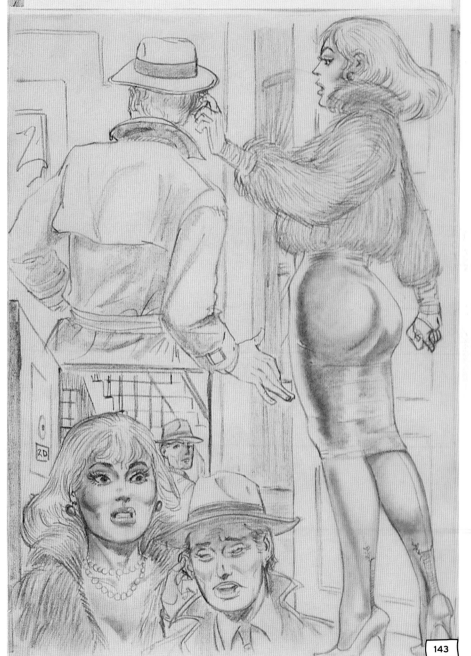

Jasper is amazed at what he has just seen and heard. So that's the new neighbors! But he must hurry upstairs with the frozen TV dinners and carry out his resolve regarding Laura. He finds Laura seated at the table, holding an ice-pack to her head. She is dressed in "shorty style" pajamas, exposing her long legs sexily crossed. Eyeing her shapely legs, he forgets about everything he has been rehearsing all day. It's been so long since they shared the same bed!

GOING TO BED SO EARLY, DEAR

YES - I'VE GOT ONE OF MY DAMN MIGRAINE HEADACHES. YOU'LL HAVE TO COOK YOUR OWN DINNER. HEAT UP ONE OF THOSE TV DINNERS. OH, WHILE IT'S ON THE STOVE, RUN DOWN TO MCENNERS'S PHARMACY AND RENEW MY HEADACHE PRESCRIPTION - I'VE RUN OUT, AND MY HEAD IS KILLING ME!

Suddenly the air is split with the sound of the radio blasting punk rock music from the apartment below. Laura jumps up enraged.

IT'S THAT CRAZY NEW COUPLE, PLAYING THEIR CRAZY MUSIC AGAIN.. JUST WHEN I'VE GOT THIS SPLITTING HEADACHE.

DON'T WORRY, DEAR..I'LL STOP BY ON MY WAY TO THE DRUG STORE AND ASK THEM TO PLEASE TURN IT OFF.

DON'T ASK THEM TELL THEM!

YES DEAR!

Jasper hurries to put one of the TV dinners on the stove. On his way out he pauses to give his wife a gentle massage on her neck and shoulders.

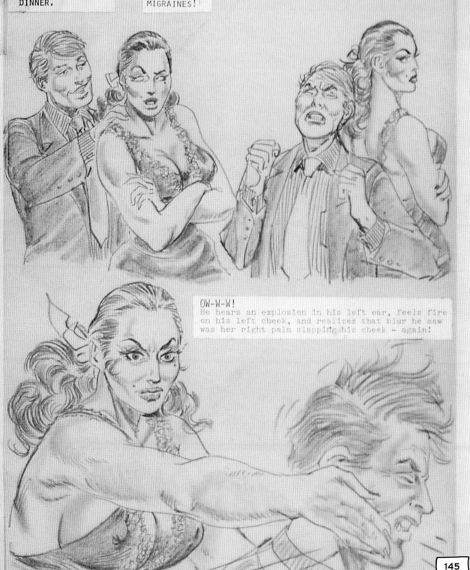

DOES THIS FEEL GOOD?

YES, BUT I NEED MY MEDICINE-- GET SOME CHOCOLATES TOO--

DAMN IT, LAURA! ITS BEEN TWO WEEKS, AND I'M SICK AND TIRED OF...

WELL, YES,...BUT IT'S REALLY NONE OF MY BUSINESS..

YES, DEAR, RIGHT AWAY, DEAR, OH, BY THE WAY, I'M TIRED TOO,SO I THINK I'LL TURN IN EARLY AS WELL. I'LL JOIN YOU RIGHT AFTER DINNER.

NO YOU WON'T YOU KNOW I MUST SLEEP ALONE WHEN I HAVE THESE MIGRAINES!

OW-W-W!
He hears an explosion in his left ear, feels fire on his left cheek, and realises that blur he saw was her right palm slapping his cheek - again!

YOU WERE SAYING, DEAR?
N-NOTHING DEAR. I-I THINK I'D..I'D BETTER GO FOR THE MEDICINE...
YES, I THINK YOU'D BETTER TOO.. ..WELL?...GET GOING!
On his way downstairs, Jasper holds his tender cheek, and curses his failure of nerve. After all his fine scheming and planning, the result was the same after all..getting his face cracked again! As he approaches the Johnson's door, that damned radio is still blasting away. He decides to put a stop to the noise. He taps on the door...No reply...He notices the door is not locked...
2D

He pushes it open just far enough to get his head in. The room is empty, but the noise is deafening. He steps inside cautiously. The noise is coming from the master bedroom. But what's that <u>other</u> noise - that odd slapping sound - crisp and rhythmic - each slap seemingly followed by a whimpering moan or yelp? Yet the slapping noise sounds familiar - where has he heard it before? Puzzled, he approaches the door, pushes it open and pokes his head in. Then he stands, transfixed, at what he sees!

A woman is seated at the far side of the bed. No mistaking that gorgeous back view - it's Mrs. Johnson. Across her lap is Mr. Johnson. With her left hand she press down his head, her fingers twined in his hair. Her right hand holds a large broad paddle high overhead, then brings it slashing down repeatedly.

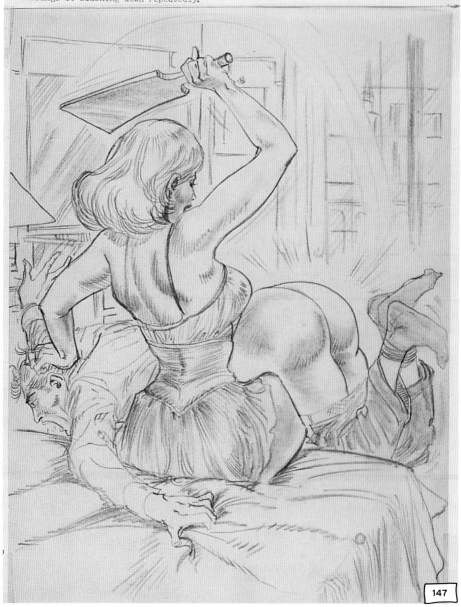

Jasper stares at Mrs. Johnson's whiplashing arm, at Mr. Johnson's jerking head to her left, howling and sobbing, and to her right, his bare thighs and kicking legs. His pants and shorts have been lowered to his knees but during his agonized kicking they have gradually worked their way down to his calves. Jasper can't see his buttocks, but he can well imagine their condition. All the while, she is sermanizing her husband.

THERE! CRACK! AND THERE! CRACK!
IT HURTS, DOES IT? WHAT DID YOU EXPECT,
YOU SILLY ASS? CRACK! HOLD STILL AND
TRY TAKING IT LIKE A MAN.
CRACK! CRACK!

DID I OR DID I NOT WARN YOU
BEFORE ABOUT FLIRTING WITH THAT
SIMPERING BLOND WAITRESS? CRACK!
HOW DARE YOU CARRY ON WITH HER
AGAIN? CRACK! NO, I'M NOT
THROUGH YET. CRACK! YOU'VE ONLY
HAD HALF YOUR DOSE! CRACK! AND
THIS IS ONLY THE FIRST
INSTALLMENT.
CRACK!

I'LL SEE TO IT YOUR ASS WILL BE RED-HOT AND BLISTERED ALL WEEK! CRACK! ARCH IT UP HIGHER! CRACK! DON'T LET IT SAG, YOU JACKASS. CRACK! CRACK! CRACK! CRACK!

ALL RIGHT... GET UP!
STAND IN THAT CORNER
AND STICK YOUR NOSE
IN AS FAR AS IT WILL
   GO.

Pointing to the corner, Laura catches
a glimpse of Jasper, unable to move, still
watching the scene. She rises slowly and
imperiously and faces the intruder.

WHO ARE YOU!?

..WHAT ARE YOU
   DOING IN MY
   BEDROOM?

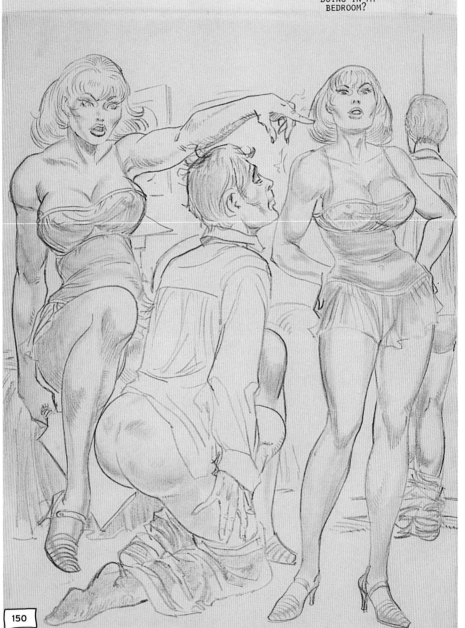

I..I..I'M JASPER PENROSE..I LIVE IN THE APARTMENT ABOVE..AND..AND..

AND YOU... ARE A PEEPING TOM.

REALLY, MA'AM...I WASN'T INVADING YOUR PRIVACY. I HAVE TO GET MEDICINE FOR MY WIFE..AND YOUR RADIO WAS DRIVING HER CRAZY... SHE HAS THIS TERRIBLE HEADACHE...

NO, NO, NO.. PLEASE...I I JUST CAME TO ASK YOU TO LOWER THE RADIO... THE DOOR WAS OPEN...

AND THAT GIVES YOU THE RIGHT TO PUSH YOUR WAY IN AND INVADE OUR PRIVACY, DOES IT?

POOR GIRL!

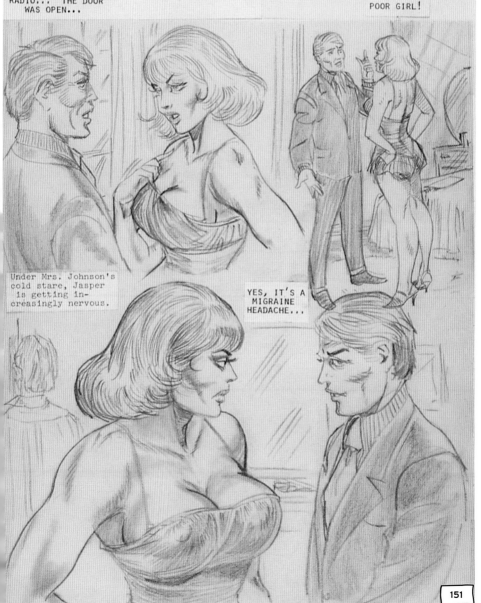

Under Mrs. Johnson's cold stare, Jasper is getting increasingly nervous.

YES, IT'S A MIGRAINE HEADACHE...

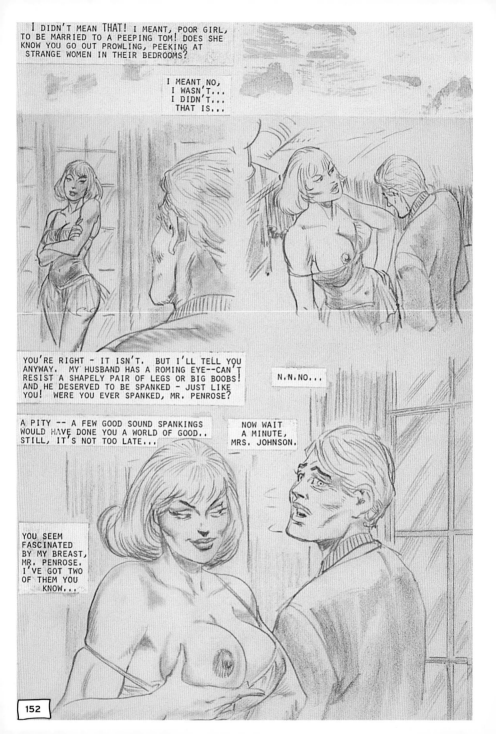

I DIDN'T MEAN THAT! I MEANT, POOR GIRL, TO BE MARRIED TO A PEEPING TOM! DOES SHE KNOW YOU GO OUT PROWLING, PEEKING AT STRANGE WOMEN IN THEIR BEDROOMS?

I MEANT NO, I WASN'T... I DIDN'T... THAT IS...

YOU'RE RIGHT - IT ISN'T. BUT I'LL TELL YOU ANYWAY. MY HUSBAND HAS A ROMING EYE--CAN'T RESIST A SHAPELY PAIR OF LEGS OR BIG BOOBS! AND HE DESERVED TO BE SPANKED - JUST LIKE YOU! WERE YOU EVER SPANKED, MR. PENROSE?

N,N,NO...

A PITY -- A FEW GOOD SOUND SPANKINGS WOULD HAVE DONE YOU A WORLD OF GOOD.. STILL, IT'S NOT TOO LATE...

NOW WAIT A MINUTE, MRS. JOHNSON.

YOU SEEM FASCINATED BY MY BREAST, MR. PENROSE. I'VE GOT TWO OF THEM YOU KNOW...

She shrugs her shoulders letting the flimsy negligee slide down both arms, completely
exposing her upper torso. Jasper almost has a heart attack.

AFTER I SPANK MY HUSBAND, AND HE
COMPLETES HIS HOUR IN THE "MEDITATION
CORNER", I ALWAYS SOOTHE AND COMFORT
HIM...I HOLD HIM CLOSE...HE SUCKS MY
TITS...IT COMFORTS HIM MARVELOUSLY...
DOESN'T IT...STEPHEN?

From her husband, standing in the "Meditation
Corner", nose pressed flat, blazing ass-cheeks
still exposed, comes a muffled response...

YES,
DEBRA
DEAR!

Debra throws her shoulders back, lifting her
massive beauties into even greater prominence.
Jasper's eyes widen and he licks his lips.
Her magnificent body so gloriously displayed
before him fills him with desire...especially
having been frustrated so long by Laura.

I'LL COMFORT YOU THE SAME WAY, MR. PENROSE...
AFTER I'VE SPANKED YOU....OF COURSE....

S.S...S..
S.PANKED ME?

IT, YOU KNOW. WELL, MR. PENROSE..
JASPER...WOULD YOU LIKE TO SUCK
MY TITS AFTER I GIVE YOU YOUR
SPANKING".

B-BUT WON'T
HE OBJECT....

SEEE.. HE
DOESN'T OBJECT.

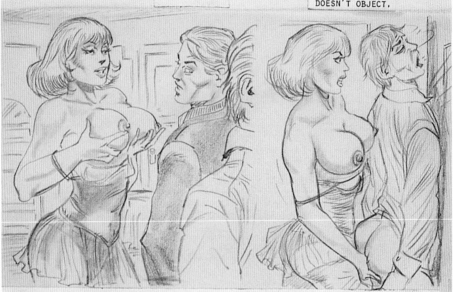

Debra re-adjusts her negligee over her breasts. She reaches out and takes him
gently by the ear. Her strong, exotic perfume fills his head. He is completely under
her spell. The fingers holding his ear pulls delicately. She moves toward the bed,
carrying him in tow. She stops by the dresser, picks up a large thick long-handled
wooden hair brush...she murmers...

FOR YOUR FIRST
SPANKING A HAIR
BRUSH IS BEST!

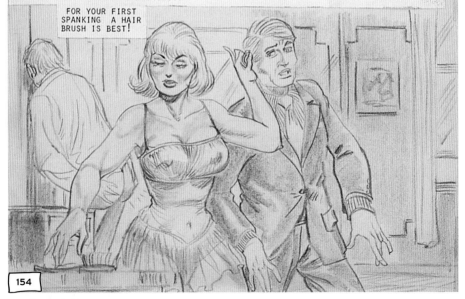

She tosses the hair brush upon the bed and takes out a length of cord from the dresser.

HANDS BEHIND YOUR BACK, JASPER!

In his dazed condition, he lets her tie his hands behind him at the wrists.

JUST SO YOU DON'T EVEN
THINK OF REBELLING.....

146

She seats herself on the edge of the bed.

COME HERE, JASPER...
STAND BESIDE MY THIGHS.

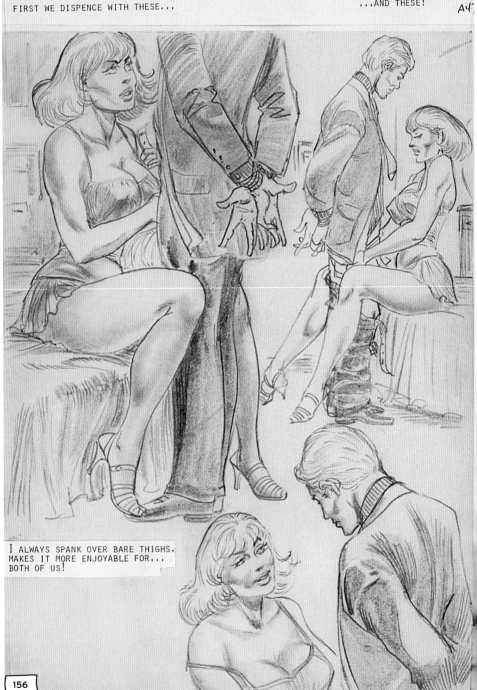

I ALWAYS SPANK OVER BARE THIGHS, MAKES IT MORE ENJOYABLE FOR... BOTH OF US!

B24

SILLY QUESTION! YOU
DON T OBJECT DO YOU,
STEPHEN?

NO!
DEBRA..
DARLING.

She steps closer, her full breasts are
thrust right before his eyes. Her negligee
happens to shift, exposing a rosy nipple...

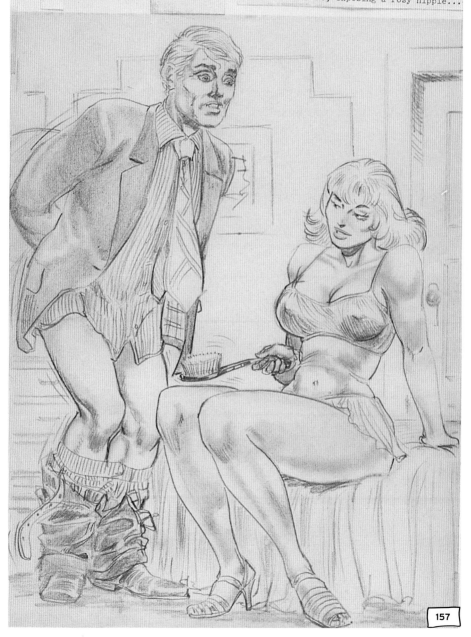

WE'LL JUST PULL UP YOUR SHORTS
SO THEY STRADDLE YOUR THIGHS...JUST
TO KEEP YOU FROM KICKING TOO HARD.

RAISE YOUR RUMP JUST A
TEENSY BIT HIGHER...THAT'S
ABOUT IT...RELAX NOTHING
HAS HAPPENED YET....

B25

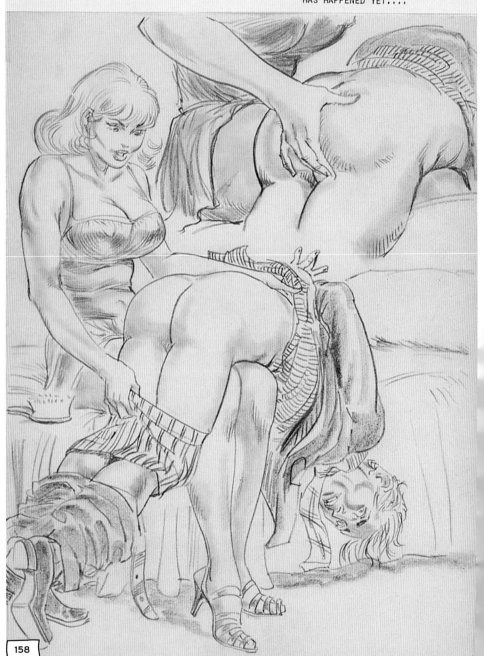

She flips his shirt-tail up over his arched rump, and he blushes as he feels the rush of cool air over the exposed skin of his cheeks. She tucks him in snugly with her left arm and with her right picks up the hair brush and raises it high overhead...the skin of his cheeks twitch uncontrollably in fearfulanticipation...

DOES THAT TEACH YOU?
AND THIS CRACK!

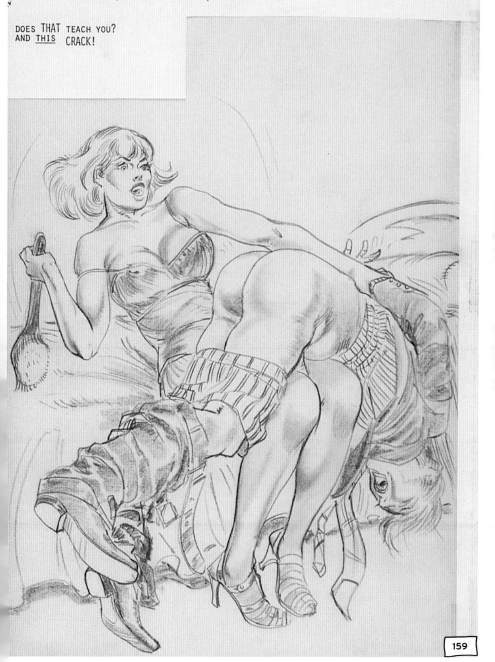

..AND THIS...NOT TO PEEK AND SPY
ON YOUR NEIGHBORS? MAYBE THIS (CRACK)
WILL TEACH YOU NOT TO GO PROWLING ABOUT
LIKE A THIEF IN THE NIGHT..CRACK..CRACK..
CREEPING INTO MY BEDROOM.. WATCHING ME
UNDRESS..CRACK...DROOLING AND SLOBERING
OVER MY BODY. (CRAAK)

B27

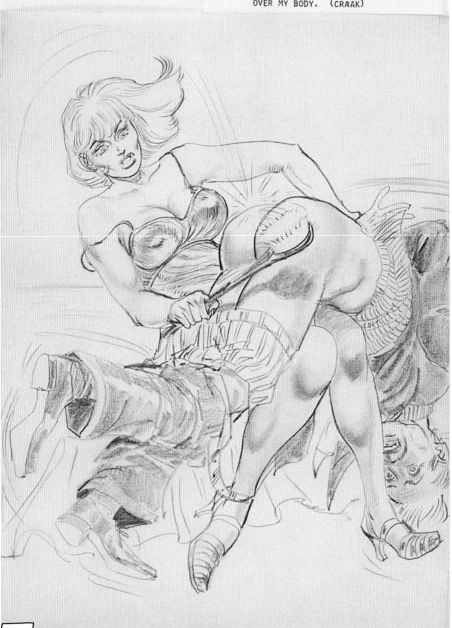

OHHH-H OW-W-W OH PLEASE MRS. JOHNSON.. MA-AM... YOU'RE TAKING THE SKIN OFF!OHH-H IT BURNS!

STEPHEN, COME OUT OF YOUR CORNER AND TURN UP THE VOLUME ON THE RADIO. HE'S YELLING TOO LOUD AND HIS WIFE MIGHT HEAR.

YES, DEAR...ER.. THAT'S AS HIGH AS IT WILL GO ...DEBRA ..DARLING....

VERY WELL STEPHEN, YOU MAY FOLLOW YOUR NOSE BACK INTO ITS CORNER....HANDS UP ABOVE YOUR HEAD, STAND STRAIGHTER, DEAR, CONTINUE MEDITATING ON YOUR MIS-BEHAVIOR WHILE I FINISH OFF MR, PENROSE HERE.

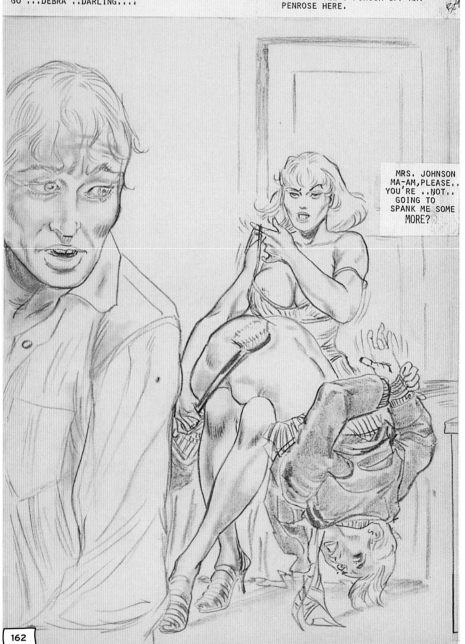

MRS, JOHNSON MA-AM, PLEASE.. YOU'RE ..NOT.. GOING TO SPANK ME SOME MORE?

162

FRAID SO, JASPER. I'M GOING TO MAKE
SURE YOU REALLY LEARNED YOUR LESSON!

WRIGGLE BACK OVER MY LAP, YOU NAUGHTY
BOY...DON'T PUCKER UP LIKE THAT...IT
ONLY HURTS MORE WHEN YOU KNOT UP THOSE
ASS-MUSCLES ... RELAX...

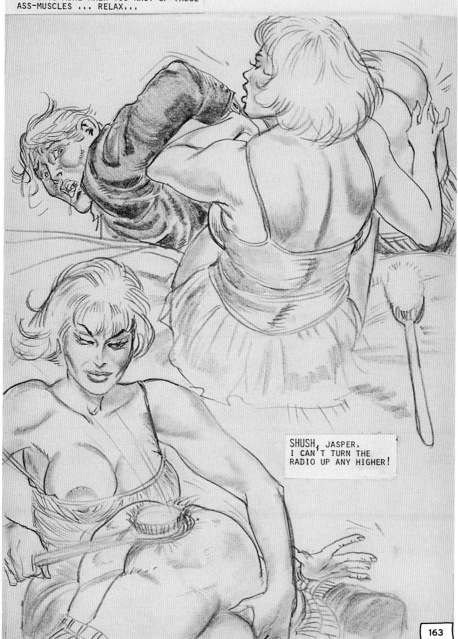

SHUSH, JASPER.
I CAN'T TURN THE
RADIO UP ANY HIGHER!

163

NOW THAT'S WHAT I CALL
A WELL-ROASTED RUMP! IT
MATCHES MY HUSBAND'S
EXACTLY...

ALL RIGHT, JASPER, GET UP
AND JOIN STEPHEN. STAND BE-
SIDE HIM AND THINK ABOUT IM-
PROVING YOUR BEHAVIOR IN
THE FUTURE.....

B31

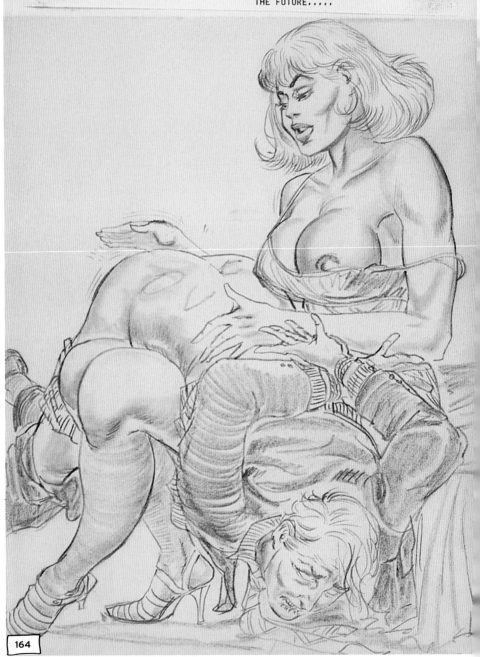

PLEASE, MRS, JOHNSON...MY WIFE'S MEDICINE ...
IT'S GETTING LATE....

OH VERY WELL, LET'S SKIP THE MEDITATION
HOUR THIS TIME. BUT I DID PROMISE TO COMFORT YOU,
DIDN'T I...KNEEL DOWN IN FRONT OF ME DEAR...

B32

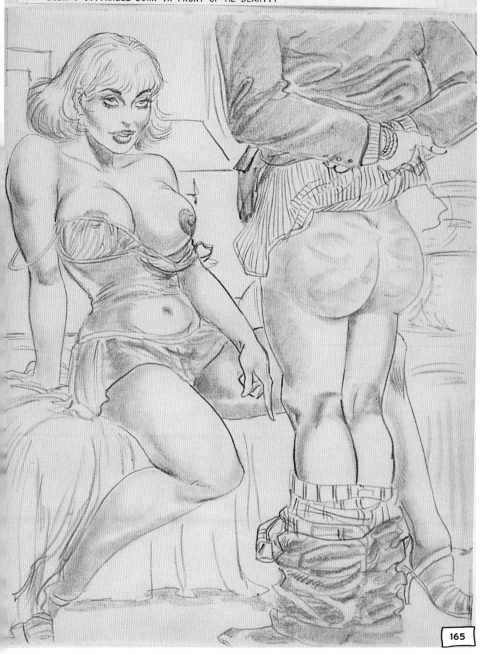

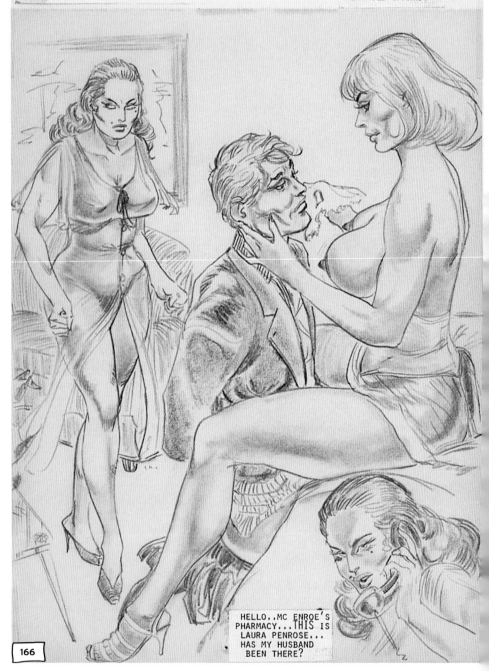

WHERE IS THAT HUSBAND OF MINE!
SO HELP ME JASPER, WHEN I GET MY
HANDS ON YOU....

SUCH A FUSS OVER A
FEW MILD SPANKS!

B33

HELLO,.MC ENROE'S
PHARMACY...THIS IS
LAURA PENROSE...
HAS MY HUSBAND
BEEN THERE?

166

Holding him by the ears she draws him closer...

WHY JASPER, YOU SEEM TO LIKE HAVING
YOUR EARS PINCHED!....YOUR MOUTH, JASPER...
HERE!

B34

Upstairs, Laura is on the telephone
again with the pharmacy ....

THANKS, MR. MC ENROE, YOU'RE VERY
KIND, BUT PLEASE DON'T KEEP OPEN ON
MY ACCOUNT. NO, I STILL DON'T KNOW
WHAT HAPPENED TO HIM, BUT I'M SURE
HE'LL HAVE A GOOD EXPLANATION...
THANKS AGAIN....

YOU'D BETTER HAVE A GOOD
EXPLANATION, JASPER PENROSE!

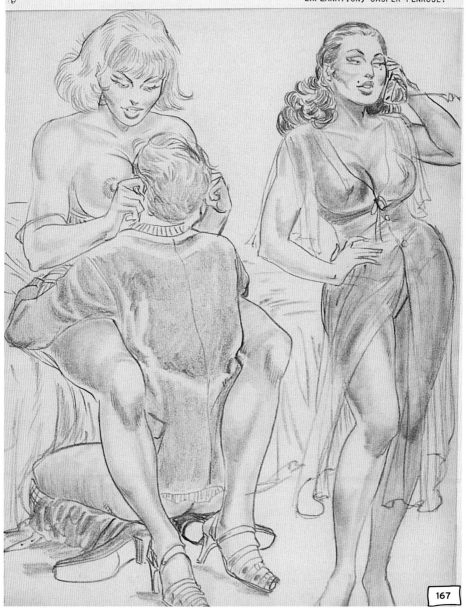

167

A half hour later (blissful half hour)
Jasper tears himself away from those melon-
like breasts.

MY GOD!   TOO LATE! THE
LAURA'S   DRUG STORE IS
MEDICINE!   CLOSED BY NOW.

Debra helps him get dressed,(she
laughs at his exclamation of pain when
he pulls up his pants over his bottom)
and offers him a bottle of asperin
for Laura's headache.

SORRY..NO TV DINNER
TO GIVE YOU BUT I DO
HAVE A SMALL PACK
OF M&MS...PLAIN.

B35

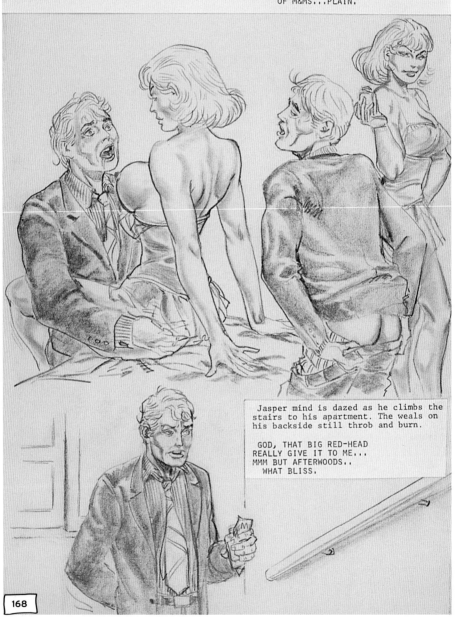

Jasper mind is dazed as he climbs the
stairs to his apartment. The weals on
his backside still throb and burn.

GOD, THAT BIG RED-HEAD
REALLY GIVE IT TO ME...
MMM BUT AFTERWOODS..
WHAT BLISS.

168

SO YOU FINALLY FOUND YOUR WAY HOME! WHAT HAPPENED?
N-N-N-NOTHING,DEAR..
836
WHY ARE YOU SO DAMN NERVOUS? WHAT HAVE YOU BEEN UP TO?
N-N-N-NOTHING, DEAR...
IS THAT ALL YOU CAN SAY, STUPID? WHERE'S MY MEDICINE?
HERE, DEAR. I GOT YOUR CHOCALATE, TOO..
IS THIS YOUR IDEA OF A JOKE, JASPER? WHERE'S THE PRESCRIPTION I SENT YOU TO GET?
ER, AHH.. THEY WERE ALL OUT OF THE INGREDIENTS DEAR. AND IT WAS TOO LATE TO SEND FOR MORE...SO I GOT THE ASPIRINS INSTEAD.
AND I SUPPOSE THEY WERE ALL OUT OF MY CHO-CALATE, TOO?..
Y-YES, DEAR.

LISTEN, JASPER. I CALLED MC ENROE'S AS SOON AS YOU LEFT, AND GAVE THEM THE PRESCRIPTION NUMBER, TO SAVE TIME. THEY'VE HAD MY MEDICINE AND BOXED CHOCALATES READY AND WAITING FOR YOU ALL THIS TIME. I KEPT CALLING THE ENTIRE TWO HOURS YOU WERE GONE. THEY SAID YOU WEREN'T THERE AT ALL. THEY SAID YOU NEVER SHOWED UP. CARE TO EXPLAIN THAT, JASPER?...

WELL...? I THOUGHT I ASKED YOU A QUESTION. I'M WAITING... OR DO I SLAP THE DAYLIGHTS OUT OF YOU TO GET AN ANSWER?

B3

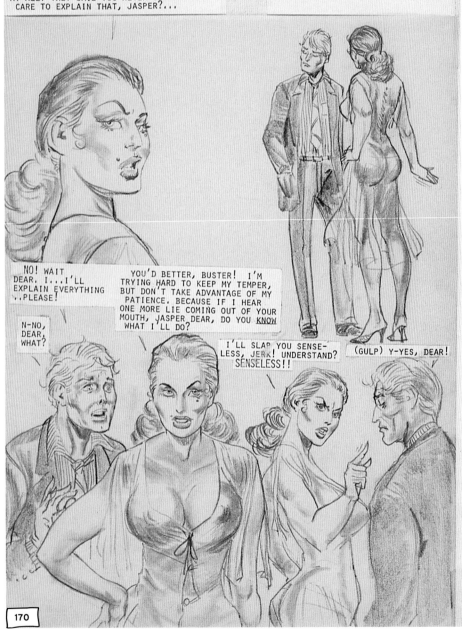

NO! WAIT DEAR. I...I'LL EXPLAIN EVERYTHING ..PLEASE!

YOU'D BETTER, BUSTER! I'M TRYING HARD TO KEEP MY TEMPER, BUT DON'T TAKE ADVANTAGE OF MY PATIENCE. BECAUSE IF I HEAR ONE MORE LIE COMING OUT OF YOUR MOUTH, JASPER DEAR, DO YOU KNOW WHAT I'LL DO?

N-NO, DEAR, WHAT?

I'LL SLAP YOU SENSE-LESS, JERK! UNDERSTAND? SENSELESS!!

(GULP) Y-YES, DEAR!

170

VERY WELL ... START FROM THE BEGINNING... WHERE THE HELL WERE YOU FOR THE PAST TWO HOURS?
WELL, ON MY WAY OUT, I PASSED THE JOHNSON'S APARTMENT AND STOPPED BY TO ASK THEM TO LOWER THEIR RADIO. I KNOW THE NOISE WAS TROUBLING YOU AND BAD FOR YOUR HEADACHE, AND I WANTED IT TURNED OFF...
HOW VERY CONSIDERATE OF YOU. BUT THEY'VE ONLY JUST TURNED DOWN THE VOLUME A FEW MINUTES AGO...JUST BEFORE YOU CAME BACK...
ER..I CAN EXPLAIN, DEAR. I STOPPED TO TALK A BIT, AND...
YOU WHAT?
I STOPPED TO CHAT WITH MR. JOHNSON..
WHAT ABOUT?
WHAT ABOUT?...ER, LET ME THINK...OH YES...I DIDN'T KNOW IT, BUT MR. JOHNSON IS BIG IN ADVERTISING, AND I THOUGHT HE COULD GIVE ME SOME ...POINTERS...

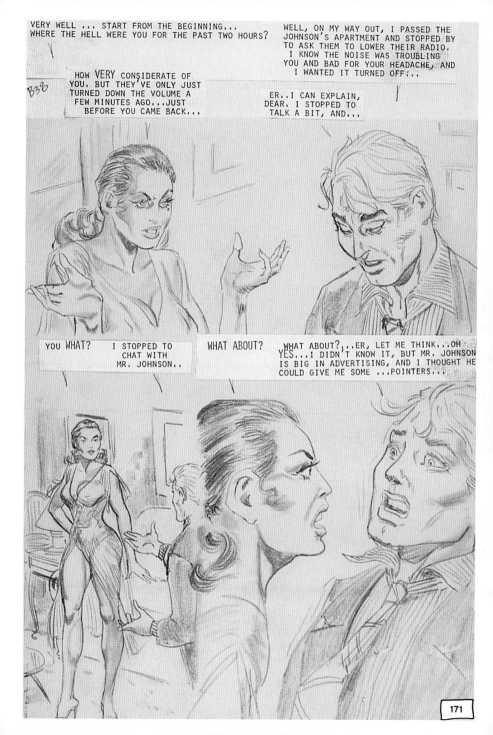

LET ME UNDERSTAND THIS. I'M WAITING FOR MEDICINE FOR MY MIGRAINE HEADACHE, WHICH IS DRIVING ME CRAZY, AND YOU STOP TO TALK ABOUT ADVERTISING?

YES! MR. JOHNSON KNOWS A LOT ABOUT ER..ADVERTISING.

YOU HAVEN'T MENTIONED MRS. JOHNSON. WASN'T SHE THERE?

WELL, YES, DEBRA...I MEAN, MRS. JOHNSON WAS THERE TOO, BUT SHE DIDN'T JOIN THE DISCUSSION AT ALL!

MY, IT MUST HAVE BEEN A LIVELY DISCUSSION. YOUR CLOTHES AND HAIR ..MESSY! SURE SHE DIDN'T JOIN IN?

OH NO! DEBRA-I MEAN, ..MRS. JOHNSON... I MEAN SHE WASN'T..

WHAT'S THAT HANDKERCHIEF DOING IN YOUR SHIRT POCKET? NO, DON'T YOU DARE TURN AWAY FROM ME! GIVE ME THAT ... HANDKERCHIEF!!

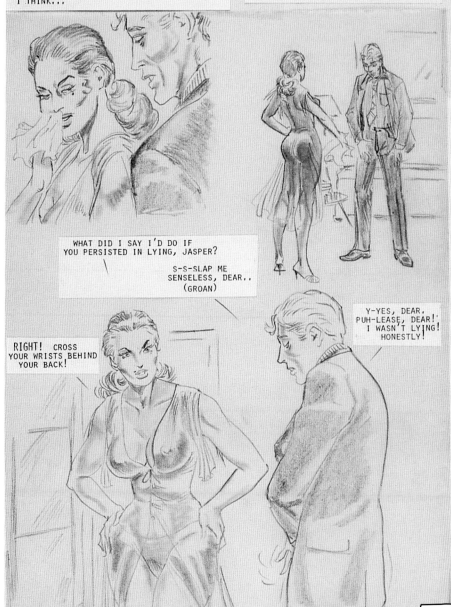

MY, THAT'S A NICE
SHADE OF LIPSTICK MR.
JOHNSON USES. I'D GUESS
HE'S A RED-HEAD. AM I
RIGHT?...SNIFF... AND
SUCH A LOVELY EXPENSIVE
PERFUME. MR. JOHNSON
USES..CHANEL NO. 5,
I THINK...

IT'S DEBRA'S
HANDKERCHIEF,...
PRECIOUS,..BUT IT'S
NOT WHAT YOU THINK,.
I CAN EXPLAIN...

I'M SURE YOU CAN! YOU'RE VERY GOOD
AT EXPLAINING, JASPER. LIKE WHERE'S MY
MEDICINE..AND WHERE YOU GOT THIS, THIS
HANDKERCHIEF..AND WHY YOUR FLY IS OPEN
AND WHY YOUR SHIRT-TAILS ARE OUT!

WHAT DID I SAY I'D DO IF
YOU PERSISTED IN LYING, JASPER?

S-S-SLAP ME
SENSELESS, DEAR,.
(GROAN)

RIGHT! CROSS
YOUR WRISTS BEHIND
YOUR BACK!

Y-YES, DEAR,
PUH-LEASE, DEAR!'
I WASN'T LYING!
HONESTLY!

173

HA! YOU DON'T KNOW THE MEANING OF THE WORD! NOW BEND OVER!
NOW HOLD YOUR FACE JUST LIKE THAT, SO I CAN SLAP IT PROPERLY.....
PAT PAT

DAMN! NOW WHO CAN THAT BE?...JASPER...FREEZE!

WHO'S THERE?

WHAT THE HELL DO YOU WANT?

STEPHEN JOHNSON, YOUR DOWNSTAIRS NEIGHBOR..MAY I COME IN A MOMENT?

SORRY TO INTRUDE, BUT MY WIFE TOLD ME TO SPEAK TO YOU ABOUT..ER, EXCUSE ME, BUT WHY IS HE STANDING LIKE THAT, IN THAT FUNNY POSITION...?

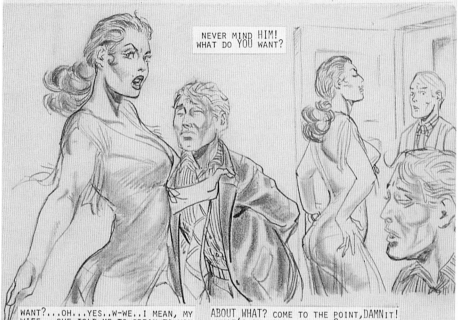

NEVER MIND HIM! WHAT DO YOU WANT?

WANT?...OH...YES..W-WE..I MEAN, MY WIFE...SHE TOLD ME TO SPEAK TO YOU ABOUT ...ABOUT...

ABOUT WHAT? COME TO THE POINT, DAMNIT! WHAT'S ON YOUR MIND... ?

THE LOUD BOOBS..ER THAT IS, THE LOUD NOISE, MY WIFE SAYS YOU SHOULD TONE IT DOWN..THE NOISE...

WHAT?!

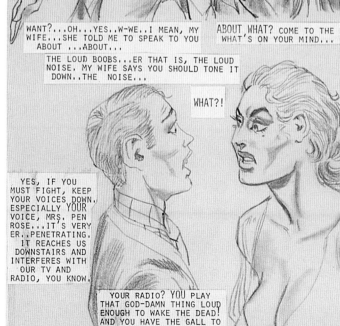

YES, IF YOU MUST FIGHT, KEEP YOUR VOICES DOWN, ESPECIALLY YOUR VOICE, MRS. PEN ROSE...IT'S VERY ER..PENETRATING, IT REACHES US DOWNSTAIRS AND INTERFERES WITH OUR TV AND RADIO, YOU KNOW.

YOUR RADIO? YOU PLAY THAT GOD-DAMN THING LOUD ENOUGH TO WAKE THE DEAD! AND YOU HAVE THE GALL TO COMPLAIN ABOUT OUR NOISE.

175

IT'S VERY RUDE OF
YOU, MRS. PENROSE, TO BE
SO INCONSIDERATE OF YOUR
NEIGHBORS...

I'M
INCONSIDERATE?
WHY...YOU-YOU..

...AND IF IT DOESN'T
STOP AT ONCE, WE'LL HAVE TO
COMPLAIN TO THE LANDLORD,
MAYBE DEMAND YOU BE
EVICTED!

B43

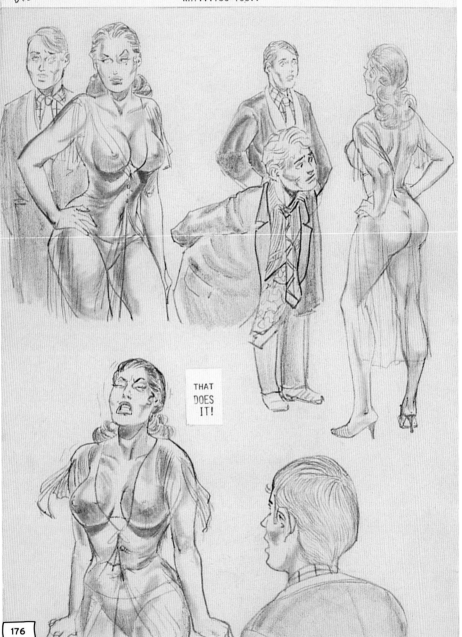

THAT
DOES
IT!

CRACK
OW-W-W-

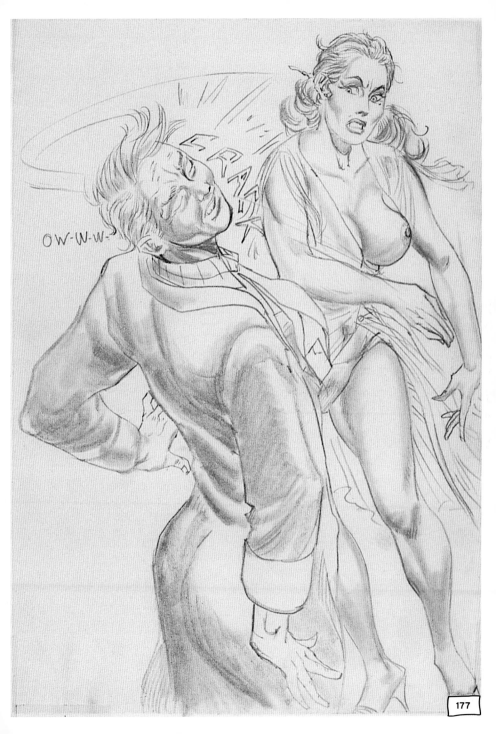

SO SHE CAN HEAR EVERY SOUND, CAN SHE? THINK SHE HEARD THAT?
WHACK
AND HOW ABOUT THIS...
CRACK

HOLD STILL, DAMN YOU!
WHAT NERVE!
B46
CRACK
WHAT GALL!..AND STOP THAT HOWLING...SHE'LL COMPLAIN ABOUT THAT TOO....

Looking on, Jasper winces in sympathy with each slap. He feels
odd, being an observer of her slapping prowess, rather than its
recipient. He is awed by her accuracy and timing..and power! if
Stephen hadn't rang the bell, that would be his teeth clenched in
pain..his face being rocked from side to side...his cheeks turning
a flaming hot red...

YOU PLAY THAT STUPID RADIO
ALL HOURS OF THE DAY AND NIGHT
AND YOU'LL HAVE US EVICTED?

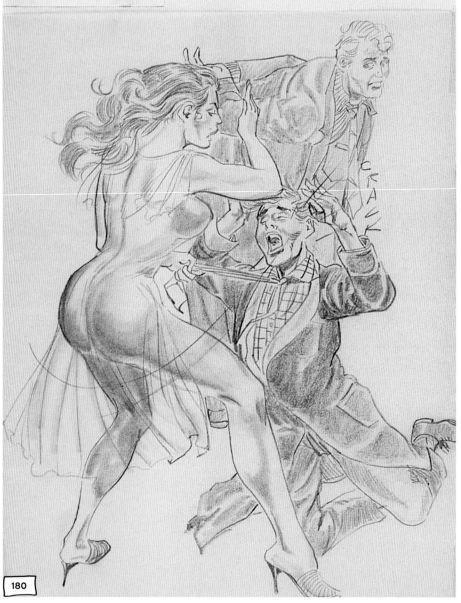

Laura emits grunting sounds with each slap. Her heavy breathing mingles with
Stephen's groans. Her beautiful hair is messed, falling haphazardly about... her
breasts jiggle loosely...(crack) She pauses to catch her breath. Stephen breaks
free and reels out the door toward the safety of his own apartment...they hear
his feet clattering down the stairs...

548

SNIVELLING COWARD!
YOU'D BETTER RUN!

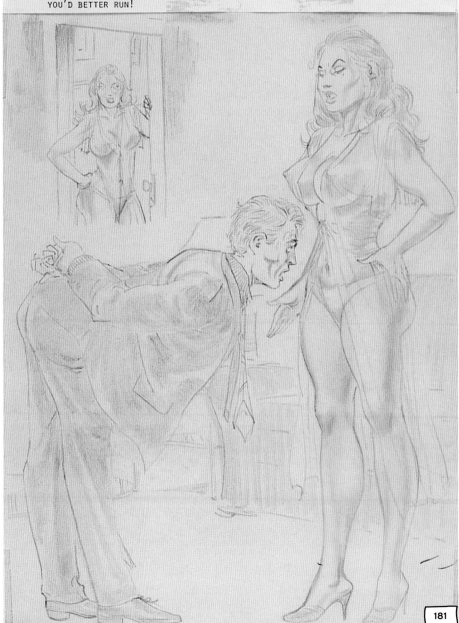

THE DOMINANT WIVES 3

ANY MORE? WHAT ARE YOU
TALKING ABOUT? I HAVEN'T
STARTED SLAPPING YOU YET!

YES DEAR... I KNOW...IT WAS
MRS. JOHNSON...SHE SPANKED SO
HARD...GOD...IT BURNS....

MRS. JOHNSON,...SPANKED YOU?
JASPER, IS THIS ANOTHER ONE
OF YOUR LIES?... TO GET OUT
OF WHATS COMING TO YOU?

NO NO NOO! HONEST DEAR. S-S-SHE MADE ME
GET OVER HER LAP..HER LAP (OH GOD) T-THEN
SHE USED A A HAIR-BRUSH...MY REAR OOH
IS STILLLL ON F-FIRE,...

NOW THIS IS INTERRESTING...PROOF IS
POSITIVE,... AND IF YOUR BUTT IS AS YOU
SAY IT IS...TURN AROUND ...BEND OVER,..
AND TAKE DOWN YOUR PANTS....DAMN!

IT'S THE DOOR BELL AGAIN.NOW WHAT? IF
IT'S THAT LITTLE WHIMPY FRIEND OF YOURS
AGAIN... I'LL REALLY GIVE HIM ....

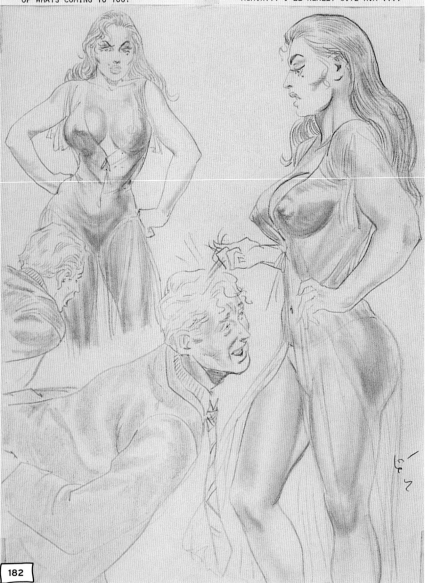

MRS. PENROSE? I AM
MRS. DEBRA JOHNSON. THIS
IS MY HUSBAND, STEPHEN.
DID YOU DO THAT TO HIS
FACE?

OF COURSE!

WHY YES OF COURSE I DID. I MOST CERTAINLY DID THAT...WHAT
YOU'RE POINTING TO. YES, YES, I AM THE ONE RESPONSIBLE FOR...
THOSE ER...DISCOLORATIONS? DID YOU DO THAT TO MY HUSBAND'S ASS?

WELL, MRS. PENROSE, MAY I CALL YOU DEBRA? IT SEEMS WE TWO
DO HAVE A LOT IN COMMON. WHY DON'T WE SIT DOWN TOGETHER AND
HAVE A NICE CHAT? I THINK WE BOTH SEEM TO HAVE A DIFFERENCE OF
OPINION ABOUT HOW TO..."HANDLE" PROBLEM HUSBANDS!

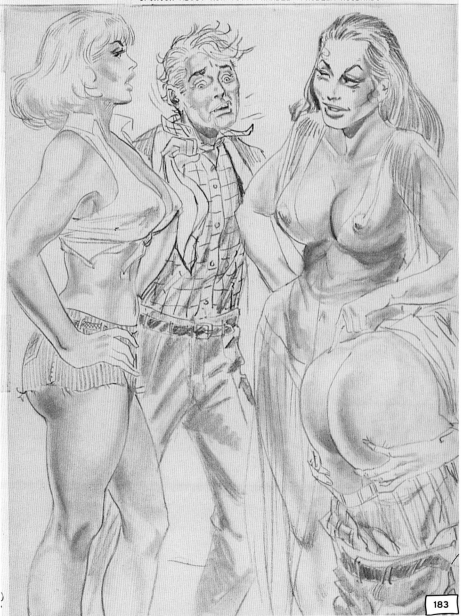

YOU SEEM TO BE DOING ALL RIGHT IN THE HUSBAND-
CONTROL DEPARTMENT BUT REALLY THERE IS NOTHING LIKE
TAKING YOUR HUSBAND'S PANTS DOWN AND TURNING HIS
 BARE ASS OVER YOUR KNEE FOR A SOUND HAIR-BRUSHING.
CAN'T YOU JUST SEE JASPER ASS-UP OVER YOUR LAP,
HEAD DOWN NEAR THE FLOOR, LOOKING BACK FOR SOME
SIGN OF MERCY, SOBBING AND PLEADING, PROMISING TO
BE GOOD? INSTEAD YOU PUT A BON-FIRE TO HIS ASS?

I'VE NEVER SPANKED JASPER, I
JUST GIVE HIM A CRACK ACROSS THE
FACE..OR TWO..OR THREE! IF I FEEL
LIKE IT...HMM...SPANKING IS SO..
CHILDISH...SO JUVENILE...BESIDES
 A SLAP IS SO QUICK...SO NEAT!

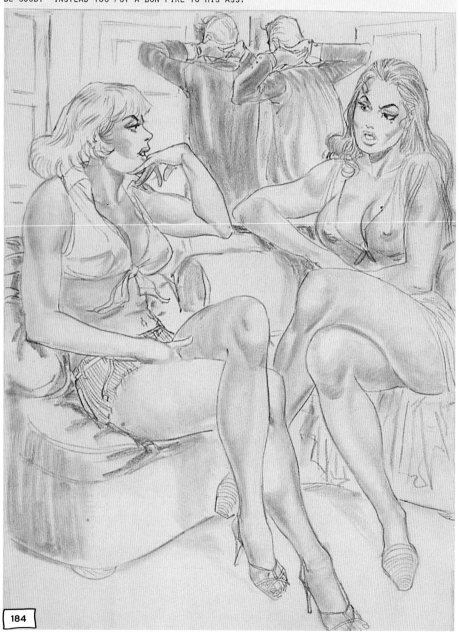

TO SETTLE THE EXISTING ARGUMENT, JASPER HAS BEEN ORDERED TO KNEEL BEFORE THE TEACHER.

VERY NICE JASPER. BUT YOU WILL HAVE TO BACK
YOUR LITTLE DERRIER UP CLOSER TO ME SO I MAY
GET A FIRM GRIP ON THE ROSY TARGET...COME NOW,
RAISE THE RUMP AND GIVE ME THE CHANCE TO PROVE
A POINT TO YOUR DOUBTING WIFE.

YOU WERE RUDE TO ME TONIGHT,
WEREN'T YOU, STEPHEN?... LIES
ABOUT LITTLE THINGS...WHEN ALL THE
TIME YOU WERE ENJOYING YOURSELF...
WITH DEBRA AND JASPER...DOWNSTAIRS.
BACK YOUR SPITEFUL ASS UP AS SHE
SAYS...NOW... YOU BASTARD!

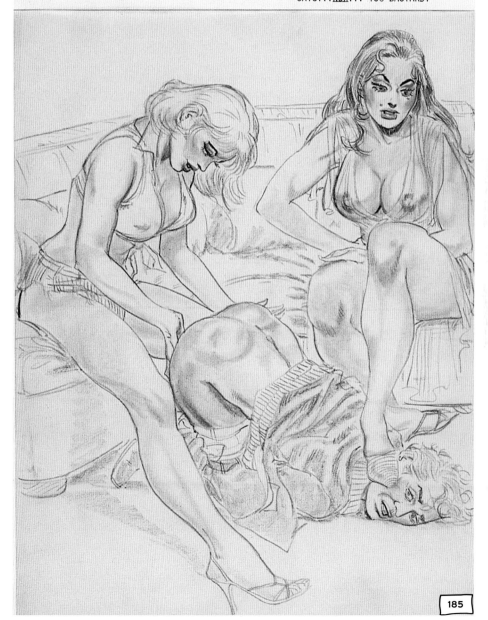

I'LL USE A NEW WEAPON UPON THIS SPOILED LITTLE MAN. HIS BELT WITH A LITTLE KNOT IN THE MIDDLE WILL HELP TO PROVE TO YOU THAT A GOOD SOUND THRASHING WITH A BELT CAN DO MORE FOR "CONTROL" THAN OTHER...

I COULDN'T DISAGREE MORE!...YOUR HUSBAND, JERKIE, IS JUST ABOUT THE WHIMPIEST EXCUSE FOR A MAN I HAVE EVER SEEN. I'M SURE THAT I CAN MAKE HIM SCREAM LOUDER THAN YOU EVER THOUGHT POSSIBLE...BEND OVER, STUPID!

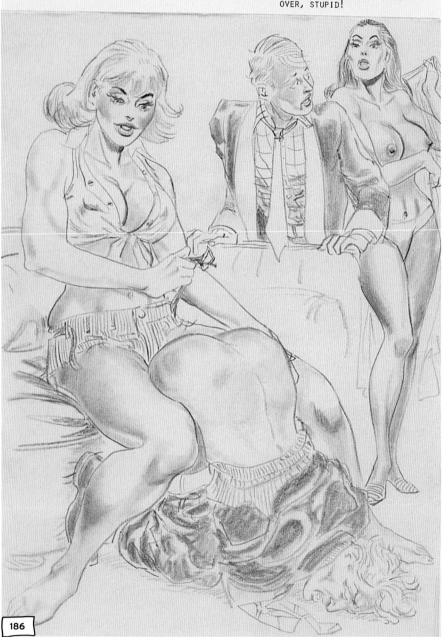

WELL...IF IT'S A CONTEST YOU ARE BEGGING
FOR...LET'S GET ON WITH IT...I SAY ..BUMMY
HERE IS THE FIRST TO CRY UNCLE...OUR WAGER
CAN BE DECIDED LATER WHEN I'VE MADE YOUR
LITTLE GIRL HERE SCREAM FIRST ...

FIRST AND LOUDEST FOR SURE WILL BE YOUR
COMPLAINING SPOUSE WHO HAD THE NERVE TO
COMPLAIN ABOUT THE NOISE...LUCKY FOR HIM HE
ISN'T DOWNSTAIRS TO HEAR THE SCREAMS OF
AGONY THAT WILL BE COMING SOON,...

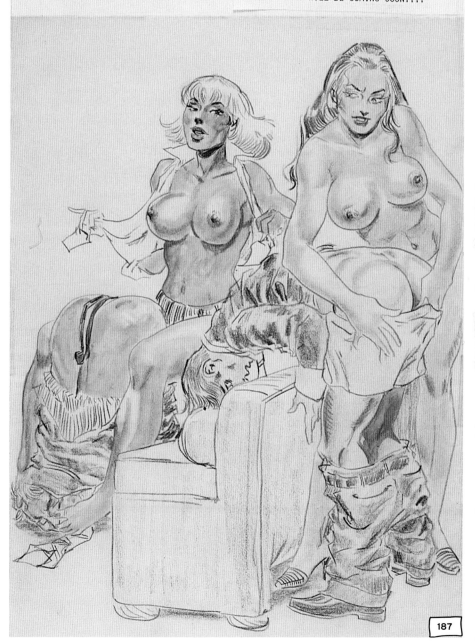

187

LET ME GET A GRIP ON THIS LITTLE THING
RESTING SO COMFORTABLE BETWEEN YOUR LEGS.
NO WONDER YOUR WIFE HAS SO MUCH NERVOUS
ENERGY...YOU DON'T DO TO WELL WITH THE
VOWS YOU ONCE MADE DO YOU...OOPS THERE
IT IS...OR IS THAT YOUR LITTLE PINKY ?
    OOHHH? YOU STILL HAVE A WARM BUTT
BUDDY...DOES MY COLD FULL BREASTS FEEL
SOOTHING TO YOUR BLISTERED, BUT NOT
    AS BLISTERED AS IT WILL BE, ASS!?

                    I MAY BE NEW AT THIS GAME OF
               ...SPANKING..BUT I TELL YOU NOT.. I
            EXPECT TO BE AN EXPERT AT IT RIGHT NOW,
            YOUR ASS CHEEKS WILL FEEL TO ME LIKE
              FOAM RUBBER COMPARED TO JASPERS FACE.
            BUT SINCE THIS IS A NEW CHEEK I DON'T
            FEEL I SHOULD USE MY HAND.. LET ME SEE
              WHAT WILL BRING OUT MORE OF YOU....

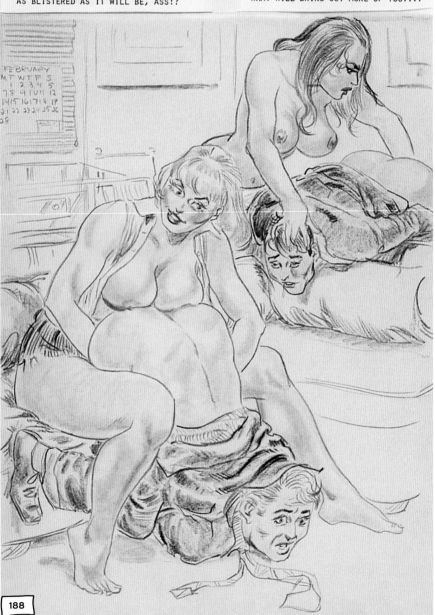

CLENCH YOUR CHEEKS IF YOU WISH JASPIE...
IT MIGHT SOFTEN THE FIRST BLOW.. BUT NOT THE SECOND ...OR THIRD OR....
FOUR (CRACK)...YOU WILL...CRY OUT!
...FIRST.(CRACK) (CRACK)

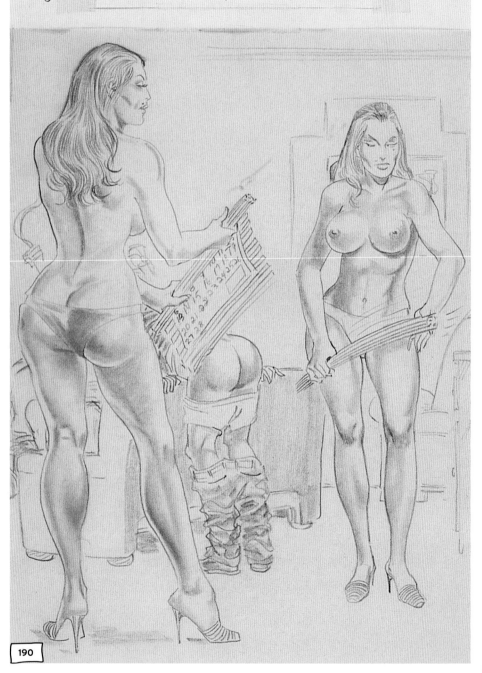

WHAT WE HAVE HERE TO FURTHER THIS CONTEST
MAY BE JUST A CALENDER BUT...IT IS A VERY STURDY
CALENDER, STEPHIE! A JAP CALENDER...YES MADE OF
BAMBOOOO...OOOH! YEP, THAT SMARTS...

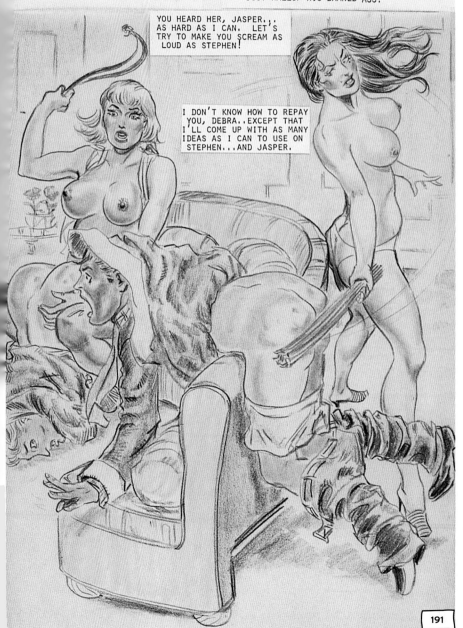

LISTEN TO HIM SQUAWK! I NEVER HEARD STEPHEN HOLLER SO MUCH. I MEAN, HE'S BEEN SPANKED SO OFTEN THAT HE'S GOOD AT HOLDING DOWN HIS REACTION, BUT YOU'VE GOT HIM SHRIEKING. LET HIM HAVE IT!

ONLY IF YOU'LL GIVE IT TO JASPER AS HARD AS YOU CAN!... THIS IS FANTASTIC! HEY! MY HEADACHE IS GONE...WOW! NOW, WHENEVER I GET A MIGRANE FROM JASPER I'LL KNOW HOW TO GET RID OF IT, I'LL JUST WALLOP HIS DAMNED ASS!

YOU HEARD HER, JASPER, AS HARD AS I CAN. LET'S TRY TO MAKE YOU SCREAM AS LOUD AS STEPHEN!

I DON'T KNOW HOW TO REPAY YOU, DEBRA,,EXCEPT THAT I'LL COME UP WITH AS MANY IDEAS AS I CAN TO USE ON STEPHEN...AND JASPER.

191

"Buy them all and add some pleasure to your life."

Art Now
Eds. Burkhard Riemschneider,
Uta Grosenick

Art. The 15th Century
Rose-Marie and Rainer Hagen

Art. The 16th Century
Rose-Marie and Rainer Hagen

Atget's Paris
Ed. Hans Christian Adam

Best of Bizarre
Ed. Eric Kroll

Karl Blossfeldt
Ed. Hans Christian Adam

Chairs
Charlotte & Peter Fiell

Classic Rock Covers
Michael Ochs

Description of Egypt
Ed. Gilles Néret

Design of the 20th Century
Charlotte & Peter Fiell

Dessous
Lingerie as Erotic Weapon
Gilles Néret

Encyclopaedia Anatomica
Museo La Specola Florence

Erotica 17th–18th Century
From Rembrandt to Fragonard
Gilles Néret

Erotica 19th Century
From Courbet to Gauguin
Gilles Néret

Erotica 20th Century, Vol. I
From Rodin to Picasso
Gilles Néret

Erotica 20th Century, Vol. II
From Dalí to Crumb
Gilles Néret

The Garden at Eichstätt
Basilius Besler

Indian Style
Ed. Angelika Taschen

Male Nudes
David Leddick

Man Ray
Ed. Manfred Heiting

Native Americans
Edward S. Curtis
Ed. Hans Christian Adam

Paris-Hollywood.
Serge Jacques
Ed. Gilles Néret

20th Century Photography
Museum Ludwig Cologne

Pin-Ups
Ed. Burkhard Riemschneider

Giovanni Battista Piranesi
Luigi Ficacci

Provence Style
Ed. Angelika Taschen

Redouté's Roses
Pierre-Joseph Redouté

Robots and Spaceships
Ed. Teruhisa Kitahara

Eric Stanton
Reunion in Ropes & Other
Stories
Ed. Burkhard Riemschneider

Eric Stanton
The Sexorcist & Other Stories
Ed. Burkhard Riemschneider

Tattoos
Ed. Henk Schiffmacher

Edward Weston
Ed. Manfred Heiting

www.taschen.com

ICONS